Recipes from the
heart of a Lebanese
city kitchen

Bayrūt
The Cookbook

Hisham Assaad

Smith
Street
Books

CONTENTS

INTRODUCTION

In this book, I want to take you on a journey into the food of Beirut. If you're a fan of Lebanese food, some recipes may be familiar to you, and some may not. I have included plenty of the best street food bites you will find around the city, as well as stews and main dishes that are traditionally cooked in homes rather than restaurants. I also share some of my favourite recipes from my own family. A few of the recipes are those fading from common use, but they are authentic to Beirut, and I wanted to archive them in this book before they are gone forever.

MY FOOD BEGINNINGS

I grew up in a food-loving family. My dad is a butcher from a family of butchers and my mom is an excellent cook, who learned from the generation preceding her, with years of practice. It was inevitable for me and my curious mind to want to get hands-on with food in one way or another. My earliest memories of food appreciation are from the time when my mom was teaching my sister how to cook, following the long-outdated expectations that girls should know how to cook. But guess who else was listening and keeping a record of the basics?

Over the years, I started trying out recipes and, through trial and error, created a repertoire of dishes that I later documented on my blog (cookin5m2.com), taking my own photos, which gradually progressed in quality. Cooking opened up opportunities I hadn't expected and I threw myself into it. It took me to many different places, such as guest cheffing at local restaurants, hosting rural tourism events, leading culinary tours, and eventually working in food styling and photography. If you're reading this book, it means I finally made it as a cookbook author (yay)!

One thing I learned from watching my mom is to cook with heart and soul. In Arabic, we call it *nafas* – a breath – and it means to put your essence into cooking. We believe that people who cook with *nafas* don't have to know the rules, yet will always make delicious food.

BEIRUT AND THE SERIES OF UNFORTUNATE EVENTS

Working on this book during a series of turbulent historic events has been difficult. The past couple of years can, at best, be described as challenging. In Lebanon, the time from late summer 2019 up to and including the coronavirus pandemic of 2020–21 has been a bumpy ride. We had the start of the economic crisis and shortages of fuel, electricity and foreign currency; the revolution came in October; we suffered inevitable inflation due to the economic measures that worsened the crisis; then came the pandemic and enforced shutdowns. To finish, the massive explosion that hit the port of Beirut on 4 August 2020, ranked among the top non-nuclear explosions in the world, crushed whatever was left of people's spirits. I turned to cooking to try to be productive or at least distract myself as the world started seemingly falling apart.

This is not something we haven't grown accustomed to. In the short lifetime of any resident of Lebanon, historic events come aplenty and we are well acquainted with tragedy. One of the major disasters that had a huge impact on the way Lebanon is today was the 15-year-long civil war. Its traces are still seen on buildings – half destroyed or marked by shells – with long-running disputes over whether they should be destroyed or preserved as heritage sites; places such as Burj El Murr, the Barakat building, the Holiday Inn, and countless more abandoned nameless buildings. We hear the stories shared by those who lived through the war and witness the traumas of the generation that came after them – the people of Lebanon were as damaged as the infrastructure.

Originally, the city of Beirut was a central point on the map of the ancient world, connecting the European, Asian and African continents, and that had a great impact on its history, culture and food. This land has been inhabited since prehistoric times – the earliest archaeological evidence goes back to the Lower Paleolithic era. The locals became known as Canaanites in the Bronze Age and Phoenicians in the Iron Age. The area has witnessed countless historic events over the centuries and millennia, and fell under the rule of many kingdoms and empires, with few windows of independence. The fight over the region between the Egyptians and the Hittites is well documented in commemorative stone slabs you will find in the region, such as two that were carved on the estuary of Nahr El-Kalb (the Dog River), a natural border of the city. It was such a hard crossing for the numerous armies that passed through this land that many of them left similar stones to mark their victories.

Beirut became part of the Greek world with the arrival of Alexander the Great, then part of the Roman Empire, becoming the first Roman colony in the East. Around the late second–early third century AD the city became a huge campus, with the installation of the first school of law, giving Beirut the title 'Mother of Laws'. The city exuded wealth with its many structures, a few of which can still be seen today (temples, forums, baths, an amphitheatre, theatre and hippodrome). It came to an end when an earthquake and ensuing tsunami destroyed the city in 551 AD. Beirut was rebuilt, but it never regained its former grandeur. A popular local legend states that Beirut was destroyed seven times, leaving seven 'stories'

under the surface. This fable was rejuvenated after the civil war with the legend of the phoenix rising from the ashes. This concept of resilience (a term I despise) became engraved in the minds of the Lebanese and is brought back with every disaster to numb the population and encourage them to accept lower living standards – it is no different today.

FOOD EVOLUTION

From the Great Famine of 1915, through civil war, revolution, pandemic, the cuisine of this region has transformed to adapt to political and economic hardships. Our food has silently evolved to represent each era. Historically, the residents of this region were farmers and sheep or goat herders. The land is bountiful, and when people slave all their lives to directly produce their food, it makes it hard for them to throw away the fruits (and vegetables) of their labour. Thus, they preserved whatever they could – in brine, vinegar, honey, sugar, fat, or under the sun, in clay pots, through fermentation, and now freezers. Cooked meals were designed around the harvest and preserves; stews were used to stretch vegetables; and salads and sides were switched up based on the seasons. Meat was a luxury reserved for special occasions – on ordinary days, a small quantity was enough to be part of the meal with vegetables, pulses and grains. Bulgur wheat was popularly consumed before rice was introduced and took over. This inherited food wisdom passed unquestioned from one generation to the next. Today, we have started re-learning why our ancestors did things in certain ways, as we discover more about food processes and their health benefits.

Lebanese food is an amalgamation of all the cultures it has interacted with. We processed the produce from the land and sea and utilised spices that came from afar. Regardless of what geographic label you want to give the region: the Middle East, Levant, eastern Mediterranean, Bilad al-Sham or the Fertile Crescent, the food of this locale was passed down through hundreds of generations, predating borders. The east coast of the Mediterranean shares very similar cuisines, but each region and every village is rich with its own varieties and specialties. For instance, you will find that Beiruti dishes differ from those prepared in Tripoli, less than 70 kilometres (40 miles) north. Despite it being hard to pinpoint the definite origin of any one recipe, it is important to me that Lebanese food is not appropriated and marketed to the West as something that it is not.

Economic hardships shift the way people consume and process foods. Now, during the times of pandemic and economic crisis, as I imagine it might have been during the Great Famine, meat has become off-limits and produce and grains are not as easily accessed by those who can't afford them – no ingredient is taken lightly. People forage when possible, try to stretch whatever they buy, and want to throw away less. I have heard of recipes prepared with mulberry and cyclamen leaves and of syrups made from the skins and peels of fruits.

This current economic crisis has fuelled the rise of local production. Knowing they can't rely on the government in our collapsed economy, citizens have resorted to self-sufficiency. Growing herbs and vegetables on balconies and in any empty plot of land is an instinctive move. The community has found ways to be sustainable, and look to directly support small producers and farmers, cut out middlemen, and try to reduce landfill by pursuing recycling and composting, which also presents an alternative to using imported fertilisers. The production and distribution of local goods has increased. Local food products – dairy, snacks, spirits and more – utilise the produce of the land, make money and sustain. I can't help but see a speck of light in terms of food innovation and recipe development from companies and restaurants trying to adapt.

GLORY TO THE CITY

My family moved to Lebanon from UAE, where I was born and raised, in 1997 and have lived there ever since, close to the hillside above the Nahr El-Kalb carved rock reliefs. A trip to Beirut was as exciting as visiting Times Square in New York. It was full of light and lively with shops, restaurants and cafes that once hosted poets, authors and journalists. It was only later that I got to know the city up close.

Like most of us living here, I have a huge love/hate relationship with Beirut. I've grown accustomed to the randomness of the city, the sight of haphazard roads and buildings, and the messy dynamics of life here. There is still a sense of organic livelihood and spontaneity among the people – it is one of the things that make living here worthwhile. That and the proximity of outstanding destinations. I could go all 'Ministry of Tourism' here with the outdated '30 minutes from skiing to swimming' slogan – a scam as it never accounted for the killer traffic – yet it *is* worth a drive for an hour or two to reach a secluded village to take your mind off reality for a while.

In 2015, I took a job with Taste Lebanon, introducing tourists to the city as a culinary guide around Beirut and few other Lebanese cities. It was never boring, despite taking almost the same route each time. The interactions with the guests always made me see a different side of the city. The streets vary and the buildings change, but you're always in for good food in any part of Beirut you're in. There are endless favourites to choose from in every corner of the city.

The city on a weekend morning is usually quiet. Nothing beats a slow walk through the alleyways and streets admiring the century-old

buildings (some even older) with their backdrops of beautiful modern architecture (or mediocre late-last-century, practical box apartments). There's a backstory, or several, to every building, and people from the neighbourhood are happy to tell you what they know. Locals are often open to chat, even with strangers, on trivial topics like the weather or traffic to deeply traumatic experiences masked as casual stories over a cup of coffee or *manouche* from a nearby bakery or a sweet treat from the famous sweet shops. My favourite walks are in spring and autumn, as the weather is cooler and less humid than it is in the summer.

When the city was divided during the civil war into West and East Beirut, the division line ran across Damascus Road all the way down to Martyrs' Square, a once lively centre known as *Sahat Al Burj*. The lower part of the 'Green Line' is dotted with drive-in shops and sandwich places, including my favourite falafel vendor. The separation no longer exists – physically at least – but is evident in the way the look and feel of the city changes. What used to be called West Beirut (my grandma still called it that) has old buildings and large colonial-style villas that are no longer in good shape and still bear bullet and shell holes from the war. The east side has changed more, as modern investment was poured into maintaining some buildings and demolishing others to erect towers. After the port explosion in 2020, many old buildings with the familiar Lebanese classical style – the 'mandaloun' three-arch façade with mullioned windows – had to be torn down for safety reasons and some were restored and renovated. People feared that the most damaged areas from the explosion would face the same destiny of gentrification that Wasat Al Balad (the city centre) faced after the civil war (bought cheaply by a big investor company from those who wanted to leave, while others were harrassed to sell or evicted, the company demolished good buildings and turned the area into a high-end residential, shopping and office district that most of the population had no access to any more). There is something heartwarming in how the older generation still call the city centre Al Balad (the nation) instead of the widely popularised name Downtown or Solidere, after the company that owns it now.

Down from Al Balad, and walking across where the beach was accessible before the expansions and illegal building, you reach the Corniche, a destination that never goes out of fashion. It is a seaside promenade that stretches across roughly 5 kilometres (3 miles) of the coastline, from the Zaytouné, with its yacht club, high-end restaurant strip and the ghost of the once internationally famous St. Georges Hotel (built in the 1920s, damaged in the civil war and whose renovation is forbidden due to Solidere's affiliations with the Beirut Municipality), all the way to the widest part at Ain Al Mraiseh, which has a huge chess board on the ground and mosaic-covered benches along the way. Looking down from the side-rails, you can't miss the many fishermen passing the time, or the hunky men perfecting their golden brown tan on any given day of the year or competing in steamy games of tennis against the older men who are always showing off. The walk continues to the amusement park and the new colourful Manara (lighthouse) – the old black-and-white striped Manara hides behind the Pink House with its many arches around the balcony. Walking further, the Corniche reaches the famous Pigeon Rock or Sakhret El Raouche (Raouche Rock), a weird evolution of the name *roche* which means 'rock' in French. Here, you can choose to sit in a coffee shop, or have your photo taken by a man with an instant camera (a rather redundant activity since smartphones and digital cameras came in), or keep walking to reach the only sandy beach left in Beirut – Ramlet Al Bayda, which translates to The White Sand. All along the way you'll find men with large pots, pouring and selling coffee, or shacks offering quick-serve beverages, but my favourites are the carts selling boiled corn-on-the-cob, fava beans served with lemon slices and cumin, and lupin beans – all nutritious, delicious snacks to accompany an afternoon or evening walk along the promenade.

A few kilometres away from the seaside, Achrafieh is an area that contains so many hidden gems, tucked in small alleyways that are sometimes hard to find, even by locals. From low-rise buildings with styles merging traditional Lebanese, Italian and French, or Ottoman architecture, to local artists' workshops under the ground-floor arcades of buildings, to artisans, vintage thrift and antique shops, or bars and restaurants in the trendy Gemmayze and Mar Mikhael, there is always something to discover and interesting people to talk to. This is one of the areas hugely affected by the port blast, but with the help of the community and donations the rebuilding and restorations are still active despite all the struggles.

I can't hide that I enjoy the refined side of Beirut, mainly found in Mar Mikhael, Gemmayze and Achrafieh (not to be confused with the soulless areas of Downtown Beirut and Beirut Souks). But away from that, the rustic sides of Beirut are also charming, from Al Basta, with its antique shops, to one of my favourite neighbourhoods on the northern outskirts of Beirut: Burj Hammoud. It used to be the most frequented shopping area, before malls came, and is the home of my favourite *soujok* (spicy Armenian sausages). It is a melting pot of cultures. Being outside of the main city made it a more affordable destination, attracting young Lebanese coming from the villages, Syrians and foreign workers from Southeast Asian and African countries, in addition to the Armenians who have been residents of the area for around a century. This diversity enriches Burj Hammoud with restaurants and shops offering products from all of the aforementioned countries. Despite being overthrown by malls, I still go there to eat, of course, and look

for and buy fabrics and props for my food styling. I get spices from Tenbelian, my favourite spice shop, which sources some of its spices from Anjar, a town in the Beqaa Valley where the second-largest Armenian population reside, and from Aleppo, when trading was easier.

By night, the bars are filled, even on a Monday, from happy hour until midnight. Hamra was a popular destination more than a decade ago, and a few bars still stand with a regular crowd to keep them going. Monot flourished then died out giving way to Gemmayze, that had a similar fate before becoming a restaurant district. Mar Mikhael stood its ground, with places popping up every now and then and the scenery always changing, catering for a young crowd while the older explored the quieter Badaro pubs and restaurants. I remember during the revolution days and nights that people would take a break from the crowds and grab a drink at their favourite bar nearby before going back to their spots and tents at the squares.

Whether it's day or night, this city is always bustling with life, no matter what gets in the way – a revolution to demand our rights, a global pandemic or an explosion. Life in Lebanon has not been easy, as we have not seen stability for a straight decade. But, just like the fig trees that will grow anywhere, we always find a way to come out, even from the toughest places, reach for the sun and be fruitful.

A FEW COOKING NOTES

Most of the recipes in this book are quick and easy, however a few might feel time consuming. They're worth every minute!

I have deliberately broken down the spice mixes in each recipe into individual spices – they might look daunting and you might not have them all, but don't worry if not. Some of the mixes can be replaced with Lebanese 7-spice or *baharat*, which are easy to find in supermarkets (*baharat* literally means 'spices' – I struggled with seeing that in some recipes for a long time!), but some dishes are better if you use the exact spices listed. Still, don't feel tied down to the recipe. Make adjustments to suit you – it may not be the same, but it'll still be good.

When cooking, I like to keep a small bowl each of fine salt and rock salt nearby. I love using rock salt when there's enough liquid to dissolve it into, or when making sauces and dressings, and will pound the salt with the garlic and whatever acid I'm using. Pounding and preparing the sauce in a mortar releases more aroma and I find it more enjoyable.

Whatever equipment or methods you're using, remember to enjoy what you're doing. To me, cooking is an immersive experience that utilises all of the senses. Most importantly, don't forget to keep the *nafas* (breath) and put your heart and soul into what you're preparing.

BREAKFAST & BRUNCH

In our modern, fast-paced world, breakfast is no longer a meal where people gather around a table. At least, not on a work day. But on weekends, or special holidays, or after a night out drinking and partying, a good meal of this calibre is much needed. In Beirut, the feast we prepare for breakfast isn't just one plate of a certain food, but rather an assortment of dishes packed with flavours and nutrients that will easily fill you up until lunchtime – even a late lunch or early dinner! And the breakfast table, like any other Lebanese table, is never complete without a selection of fresh vegetables and herbs, harvested in the early morning or the evening before – or, if purchased, when you can be sure that they haven't travelled far and are still at the peak of freshness.

Lebanese breakfasts rely on proteins and complex carbs from pulses and grains. Historically, meat wasn't regularly consumed because it wasn't available all the time. Of course, when an animal was butchered, fresh meat was dedicated to be served fresh first. It's not uncommon among meat lovers to serve for breakfast a platter of raw lamb cubes, fat cubes (*liyyeh*), which come from the highly prized large fatty tail of the Abou Liyyeh sheep raised in the region, and chopped liver, along with lots of fresh mint and onions and, of course, olive oil and a small side plate of salt and allspice. The feast is completed with a small glass of Lion's Milk: *arak*, a highly concentrated liquor distilled with aniseed. They say the high alcohol content of the *arak* kills any germs or bacteria in the meat.

Since I'm not including any of those local – diminishing – delicacies here, let me tell you instead about the other, rather vegetarian, breakfast feast you should have in Beirut. Abou Hassan is a hidden gem in the small streets of Burj Hammoud, a place that people frequent in the early morning hours after a night of drinking and partying, whether it be bar hopping in Gemmayze or Mar Mikhael or in the nightclubs and rooftop hangouts scattered around the capital. A humble restaurant that has been running for decades, Abou Hassan serves simple dishes, such as *fatteh* (chickpeas/garbanzo beans with garlic yoghurt and fried bread, see page 18), *ful mdammas* (broad/fava beans with garlic and olive oil, page 21) and *balila* (chickpeas/garbanzo beans with cumin, page 22) – all recipes you'll find in this chapter. Whether you're there on your own for a regular breakfast or with a group of friends, you'll be served quickly and a table of fresh produce and warm bread will be laid in front of you.

If I didn't convince you to allow me to take you to Abou Hassan, bring the flavours home and make them yourselves and I'll guide you through it. If you're organising breakfast or brunch, make at least three of the dishes on the following pages and don't forget the fresh vegetables and herbs and, of course, the fresh bread.

CHICKPEAS & GARLIC YOGHURT WITH FRIED BREAD
Fatteh

Fatteh, which comes from the Arabic for crumbling bread (*fatta al khobz*), is one of those recipes that went from being a leftovers solution to a glamorous dish. It uses stale bread that's toasted or fried and crumbled to create a base, which is then covered with yoghurt and other savoury toppings. The varieties are endless and they change based on what you have in your cupboard and what meal you're serving it for. A few years ago, a shrimp *fatteh* became the talk of the town due to someone sharing it on Snapchat among the local traditional dishes in a Lebanese restaurant. While the dish doesn't sound that bad, it surely isn't traditional.

I find this dish to be like a savoury breakfast trifle (not in a Rachel Green from *Friends* way – we're not talking meat with jam and sponge layers here!). Layer the fried or toasted crumbled bread at the bottom to soak up the delicious juices from the other ingredients and top with chickpeas and garlicky yoghurt with fried nuts for a mix of textures.

If using dried chickpeas, soak them overnight in plenty of water.

The next day, drain the chickpeas, place in a saucepan and cover with plenty of fresh water. Bring to the boil, then skim off the foam with a slotted spoon. Reduce the heat and simmer for 1–1½ hours until the chickpeas are cooked and tender. Drain, reserving ½ cup of the cooking liquid, and let cool slightly. Alternatively, drain the tinned chickpeas, reserving ½ cup of their soaking liquid, and heat through in a saucepan with the reserved liquid.

In a pestle and mortar, smash the garlic with the salt. Mix with the yoghurt.

Toast or fry the pita bread and break into large pieces. Place the pieces at the bottom of a large serving bowl and lightly soak the bread with some of the chickpea cooking liquid. (If you prefer a little crunch to your *fatteh*, reserve some of the crispy bread in a separate bowl to serve alongside.) Top with the cooked chickpeas, then drizzle over the garlic yoghurt.

Meanwhile, heat the butter/ghee and olive oil in a pan and toast the nuts until golden. Scoop the nuts and the hot butter/oil mixture over the yoghurt, dust with paprika and serve immediately.

250 g (1 cup) dried chickpeas (garbanzo beans) or 2 x 400 g (14 oz) tinned

2 garlic cloves

1 teaspoon sea salt

500 g (2 cups) plain yoghurt

50 g (2 oz) pita bread

2 tablespoons butter or ghee

1 tablespoon olive oil

50 g (scant ½ cup) cashews

50 g (⅔ cup) slivered (flaked) almonds

50 g (scant ½ cup) pine nuts (optional)

pinch of paprika, for dusting

BROAD BEANS WITH GARLIC & OLIVE OIL
Ful Mdammas

300 g (1½ cups) small dried broad (fava) beans or 3 x 300 g (10½ oz) tinned

2 large garlic cloves

1 teaspoon sea salt

5 tablespoons bitter orange juice (or more lemon juice, to taste)

3 tablespoons lemon juice

2 teaspoons ground cumin

1 teaspoon chilli powder

2 tomatoes, chopped, to garnish

small handful of flat-leaf parsley, chopped, to garnish

90 ml (generous ⅓ cup) olive oil

fresh pita bread, to serve

The traditional food of the Lebanon is peasant food, as the Lebanese relied heavily on farming and agriculture before the modern-day lure of the service industries, especially after several devastating incidents of war and famine. Pulses dried in season last for almost a year in the pantry or larder and were always the best option for winter, especially during times when refrigeration was not common. A plate of *ful* (broad/fava beans) was certain to fill you up at breakfastime and fuel you through a day working in the fields. Alternatively, it could make a filling lunch as it holds well without cooling.

The thing that sets this dish apart among Beirutis is the use of bitter orange juice with (or to replace) lemon juice when bitter oranges are in season. I always juice bitter oranges when they are in season and freeze the juice in bottles to use the rest of the year.

If using dried broad beans, soak them overnight in plenty of water.

The next day, drain the beans, then place in a saucepan and cover with fresh water. Cover and cook for 1 hour (or for 30 minutes in a pressure cooker), until tender. Drain, reserving a little of the cooking liquid. If using tinned beans, place the beans with their soaking liquid in a saucepan and heat through. Drain and reserve the liquid to use later.

Smash the garlic, pounding it in a mortar and pestle with a little of the salt.

Scoop 1 cup of the cooked, drained beans into a large bowl and mash slightly with a pestle. Season with the bitter orange juice (if using), lemon juice, the mashed garlic, cumin, chilli powder and the remaining salt. Add the rest of the beans along with 2–3 tablespoons of the cooking liquid to loosen the mixture a little and combine.

Garnish with chopped tomatoes and parsley and cover generously with the olive oil. Serve with fresh pita bread.

Note: Cooked unseasoned broad beans can be stored in the fridge or freezer if you prefer cooking a larger quantity for a quick breakfast the following day.

CHICKPEAS WITH CUMIN
Balila

A classic among the Beiruti breakfast spread dishes, warm chickpeas are seasoned with cumin and garlic and, of course, a generous drizzle of lemon and good olive oil. This is bound to make your day and is a breakfast that will fill you up past lunchtime. Serve this with a plate of *Ful Mdammas* (page 21) and plenty of seasonal veggies and herbs that are peppery and delicious, such as cress. I love to have *balila* with a side of sunny-side-up eggs and scoop it up with warm, fresh bread.

If using dried chickpeas, soak them overnight in plenty of water.

The next day, drain the chickpeas, place in a saucepan and cover with plenty of fresh water. Bring to the boil, then skim off the foam with a slotted spoon. Reduce the heat and simmer for 1–1½ hours until the chickpeas are cooked and almost falling apart. Drain and set aside to cool slightly. Alternatively, drain the tinned chickpeas, reserving a little of their soaking liquid, place in a saucepan with the reserved liquid and heat through.

In a pestle and mortar, smash the garlic with the salt and transfer to a bowl. Scoop out 1 cup of the cooked chickpeas and lightly smash in the mortar, then transfer to the bowl. Add the rest of the chickpeas along with the cumin, olive oil and lemon juice and mix to combine.

Serve while slightly warm with an extra drizzle of olive oil and a dusting of cumin and red chilli powder. Serve with soft pita bread and tomatoes, cucumbers, mint, radishes, cress, spring onions and olives, and a cup of hot tea.

Pictured on page 24.

250 g (1 cup) dried chickpeas (garbanzo beans) or 2 x 400 g (14 oz) tinned

4 garlic cloves

1 teaspoon sea salt

2 teaspoons ground cumin, plus extra to garnish

60 ml (¼ cup) olive oil, plus extra for drizzling

120 ml (½ cup) freshly squeezed lemon juice

chilli powder, to garnish

To serve

sliced tomatoes, cucumbers, mint, radishes, cress, spring onions (scallions), olives

fresh pita bread

BLACK-EYED PEAS WITH GARLIC, LEMON & OIL
Loubye Msallat Mtabbalé

300 g (1½ cups) dried black-eyed peas or 3 x 400 g (14 oz) tinned

4 tablespoons Coriander and Garlic Pesto (see page 209)

zest and juice of 1½ lemons (about 60 ml/¼ cup)

60 ml (¼ cup) olive oil

150 g (5 oz) cherry tomatoes (optional)

2 Lebanese cucumbers (optional)

sea salt, to taste

My friend Iffat, an original Beiruti, told me that this used to be one of her favourite family breakfast dishes growing up. The flavours of coriander (cilantro) and garlic are so bright and refreshing, they're bound to kickstart the day on a high note.

In this recipe, I suggest a variation that takes the dish away from being a warm bowl like the other breakfast bean dishes and into a fresh salad that can stand on its own, or be a part of the breakfast spread with sunny-side-up eggs and fresh bread and veggies. The choice is yours. You can enjoy a taste of Iffat's Beiruti breakfast any way you like.

If using dried black-eyed peas, soak them overnight in plenty of water.

The next day, drain and rinse the peas, place in a saucepan and cover with fresh water. Bring to the boil and skim off and discard the foam that rises to the surface. Reduce the heat and simmer for 20–30 minutes until cooked. Drain, reserving a little of the cooking water and set aside to cool. Alternatively, drain the tinned peas, reserving a little of their soaking liquid, place in a saucepan with the reserved liquid and gently heat through.

When cool, you can either mix the beans with the pesto and a little of the cooking water to loosen, then season with salt, lemon juice and zest and olive oil, to taste. Alternatively, if using tomatoes and cucumbers, chop them and place them in a bowl. Add the pesto, lemon juice and zest, olive oil and salt. Add the cooled peas and toss until well combined. Taste and adjust the seasoning if needed.

Serve on its own, or with bread and more fresh vegetables.

ZUCCHINI & DILL FRITTERS

Ijjeh Bil Koussa wel Shoumar

Whenever I go on hiking trips (usually during the cooler spring and autumn seasons), I'm always scanning my surroundings for edible plants. The mountains around Beirut are filled with a wide variety of fantastic edible greens, such as za'atar (wild thyme), wild garlic, sour sob, and many others. Dill weed, with its anise aroma and flavour, is particularly common in the hills and always reminds me of liquorice and *arak*, but mostly of the delicious fritters my neighbour used to make from the bunch of wild dill she would collect herself.

Place the grated zucchini in a colander, sprinkle with the salt and set over a bowl or in the sink for 10 minutes to drain off any excess water.

Put the dill and spring onions into a large bowl and crack in the eggs. Add the allspice and flour and mix to combine well.

Press as much liquid out of the zucchini as possible and transfer to the egg mixture. Mix well. Just before frying, mix in the baking powder.

Cook the fritters in batches. Heat a little olive oil in a wide frying pan (skillet) over a medium heat. Scoop ¼-cup rounds of the fritter mixture into the pan and cook for 2 minutes or until slightly browned on the bottom, then carefully flip and cook for a further 1 minute. Remove with a slotted spoon to drain on paper towels. You can place the cooked fritters in a warm oven to keep hot until serving, if you like. Continue frying until all the mixture is used up.

Serve the warm fritters with soft pita bread with a labneh and veggie dip, or yoghurt and cucumber salad, garnished with an extra touch of fresh dill.

Note: For a gluten-free version, you can replace the flour with cornflour (cornstarch).

450 g (1 lb) zucchini (courgettes), grated

2 teaspoons sea salt

60 g (2 oz) fresh dill, chopped, plus a few sprigs to garnish

50 g (2 oz) spring onions (scallions), finely sliced

6 eggs

1 teaspoon allspice

80 g (⅔ cup) plain (all-purpose) flour (see note)

1 teaspoon baking powder

olive oil, for frying

To serve

pita breads

Labneh and Veggie Dip (page 30) or Cucumber and Yoghurt Salad (page 81)

LABNEH & VEGGIE DIP
Beiruti Labneh

Labneh – a thick, strained yoghurt – is easy to make and more delicious than cream cheese due to the tanginess of the fermented yoghurt we get here. It is the reason I never considered going vegan. Basically, I am a labneh-holic and proud of it. I put labneh in and on anything. Whether it's in wrap, or *a'arous* as we call it, with cucumber and mint, on toasted sourdough bread with a little bit of basil pesto, with whipped cream for a dessert, or in cheesecake, there is always a use for labneh. Find the recipe for home-made labneh in the Basics chapter (page 216) and make this dip for breakfast, lunch, dinner, or for a healthy snack with sliced carrots or zucchini.

Very few restaurants serve this version – they serve plain labneh dip with a drizzle of olive oil or mix it with dried mint and fresh garlic for a twist. *Beiruti Labneh* is one of the dishes my dad makes so well at home for a family gathering on his day off. It barely takes any time and, as a skilled butcher, chopping a few vegetables is as easy and quick to him as a hot knife cutting through butter.

If making your own labneh, start it the night before. Refrigerate overnight.

Finely dice the cucumber. Halve and de-seed the tomato to get rid of excess liquid, then chop into small dice the same size as the cucumber. Finely chop the mint and finely slice the spring onions, both white and green parts.

Mix the chopped veg and mint with the labneh and season with salt to taste. Spread over a serving plate and generously drizzle with olive oil.

Serve with fresh or toasted pita bread, or plain tortilla chips, or with sliced carrots and zucchini.

500 g (2 cups) labneh (store-bought or home-made, see page 216)

2 Lebanese cucumbers (each about 10 cm/4 in long) or 1 regular cucumber, deseeded

1 medium tomato

large handful of mint

2 spring onions (scallions)

sea salt, to taste

olive oil, for drizzling

To serve (optional)
fresh or toasted pita bread

plain tortilla chips

sliced carrots and zucchini (courgettes)

SCRAMBLED EGGS WITH MEAT OR POTATOES
Mfarraket Lahme/Batata wa Bayd

For the potato version
8 eggs
250 ml (1 cup) olive oil
100 g (3½ oz) onion, diced
800 g (1 lb 12 oz) potatoes, diced
1 teaspoon salt, or more to taste
¼ teaspoon allspice, or more to taste

For the meat version
8 eggs
2 tablespoons olive oil
100 g (3½ oz) onion, diced
400 g (14 oz) minced (ground) beef
1 teaspoon salt, or more to taste
1 teaspoon ground cinnamon
¼ teaspoon allspice, or more to taste

To serve
sliced vegetables of choice
soft pita bread

A simple dish, this is a quick fix that my mom prepares when she hasn't planned what to cook for breakfast or lunch. What's not to like? Potatoes, good. Eggs, good. Beef, GOOD!

This also makes a great lunch, served in soft Arabic bread with a drizzle of hot sauce and wrapped up to go. If you're not in a hurry, make it the centrepiece of a breakfast or brunch feast with all the good sides: labneh, pickles, olives, mint and seasonal greens and, of course, good fresh bread.

Instead of the spices suggested here, the meat version can also be seasoned with the soujok spice mixture on page 32, for an Armenian-style flavour, or with *awarma*, a meat confit preserved in sheep's tail fat, if you can find it.

For the potato version
Crack the eggs into a large bowl, whisk and set aside.

Heat the oil in a wide frying pan (skillet) over a medium heat, add the onions and sauté until slightly softened but not coloured. Next, add the potatoes and fry until tender. Carefully drain away most of the oil (it can be used for frying in other recipes, so don't throw it away).

Pour the eggs into the pan, season to taste with salt and allspice, and cook, stirring, until firmed to your liking.

Serve with a little more allspice and a side of vegetables and soft pita bread.

For the meat version
Crack the eggs into a large bowl, whisk and set aside.

Heat the oil in a wide frying pan (skillet) over a medium heat, add the onions and sauté until slightly softened but not coloured. Add the beef, season with salt, cinnamon and allspice, and cook, stirring, until completely browned. Add the eggs and cook, stirring, until firmed to your liking.

Serve as above.

HUMMUS WITH SOUJOK-SPICED BEEF
Hummus bei Soujok

Soujok are Armenian spicy sausages (see recipe on page 73) and the flavour is so distinct that I love using them in other breakfast recipes, such as sausages and eggs on toast, or chopped up in shakshuka. Here, I have used the same spice mix to flavour the succulent meat topping that crowns this creamy hummus. Topping hummus with meat isn't uncommon in the Levant. It's a way to pump up the protein and fat in the dish and make it closer to a meal than a side dish.

This makes a larger batch of the spice mix than you will need, so store it in an airtight jar and use with any other meat dishes – in stews, or as a dry rub – or even sprinkle on popcorn. If you don't have the list of spices in your cupboard, you could substitute 3 tablespoons of baharat (Lebanese 7-spice mix) with ½ teaspoon of fenugreek to keep the distinct *soujok* flavour and aroma.

This is my mom's hummus recipe – she is known for it, so I had to share it with you. Bear in mind that everyone's taste is personal when it comes to hummus, so you can adjust it to suit your own preference. I like mine to have a distinct tahini flavour with a nice kick of lemon and prefer it without garlic, which makes it last longer in the fridge before spoiling. Hello... hummus on everything! We add the citric acid to enhance the lemony taste without diluting the hummus with a lot of lemon juice.

Soak the dried chickpeas for the hummus overnight in plenty of water.

Prepare the soujok spice mix by mixing all of the ground spices together.

In a large bowl, combine the beef, garlic, pepper paste and 3 tablespoons of the spice mix and work with your hands until it is well combined. Leave to marinate in the refrigerator for a few hours, or ideally overnight, to develop the flavour.

The next day, drain the chickpeas and place in a large saucepan, cover with fresh water and bring to the boil. Use a slotted spoon to skim off and discard the foam on the surface of the liquid. Reduce the heat and simmer for 1½–2 hours until the chickpeas are really soft and almost

For the Hummus
400 g (generous 1¾ cups) dried chickpeas (garbanzo beans)

150 g (generous ½ cup) tahini

120 ml (½ cup) freshly squeezed lemon juice

¼ teaspoon citric acid

1 tablespoon sea salt

For the Soujok
250 g (9 oz) finely minced (ground) beef (20% fat)

2 garlic cloves, minced

2 tablespoons red pepper paste

For the Soujok Spice Mix
½ teaspoon allspice

1 teaspoon white pepper

½ teaspoon black pepper

2 teaspoons ground cumin

2 teaspoons sea salt

¼ teaspoon ground nutmeg

1 tablespoon garlic powder

1 tablespoon paprika

1 tablespoon dried chilli flakes

1 tablespoon ground fenugreek

To serve
2 tablespoons olive oil (or 1 tablespoon olive oil and 1 tablespoon butter), plus extra for drizzling

50 g (scant ½ cup) whole almonds and/ or cashews

pita bread

recipe continues overleaf...›

...▸ collapsing (the exact time can vary enormously depending on the chickpeas and the mineral content of the water where you live, so keep testing them until you are satisfied). Reserve 1 cup of the chickpea cooking water, then set the whole pan under running cold water to help remove the loose chickpea skins, which will float to the top. Scoop the skins out and discard. Strain the chickpeas and allow them to cool to room temperature.

Place the cooled chickpeas in a food processor and pulse until creamy, adding a little of the cooking water to loosen, if necessary. The trick is to make them creamy before adding any further ingredients, otherwise you'll never achieve SUPER CREAMY hummus! Once the chickpeas are creamy, add the tahini, half of the lemon juice, the citric acid and the salt. Pulse to combine, then taste and adjust the flavour, adding more lemon juice to taste. A good hummus should have the perfect balance between a thick creamy texture and being smooth enough to scoop up with pita bread. It should never be runny.

In a frying pan (skillet), heat the olive oil (or oil and butter) over a medium heat. Add the nuts and fry until golden, then remove with a slotted spoon to drain on paper towels.

Add the remaining oil to the same pan, then add the meat and fry for 5–7 minutes until well browned and most of the liquid has evaporated, breaking it up into small pieces as it cooks.

To serve, place around 1 cup of hummus into a small shallow bowl and shape it into a dome with the back of a spoon or a spatula. Gently press into the middle of the dome with the spatula and spin the plate with your other hand to create a deep well in the middle. Scoop some of the warm spiced beef into the well, drizzle with olive oil and top with the golden crunchy nuts. Serve with soft or toasted pita bread, cut into triangles.

ARMENIAN SWEET TAHINI & CINNAMON BREAD
Tahinov Hatz

350 g (2¾ cups) strong (bread) flour, plus extra for dusting

1 teaspoon fine salt

1 teaspoon white caster (superfine) sugar

7 g (2 teaspoons) instant dried yeast

200 ml (scant 1 cup) room-temperature water

1 tablespoon olive oil

For the topping

135g (½ cup) tahini

100–150g (½–¾ cup) white caster (superfine) or soft light brown sugar

2–4 tablespoons ground cinnamon

Another Armenian specialty, this bread is made during Lent since it contains no animal products. You can get it from Armenian bakeries in Burj Hammoud, an area to the north of Beirut where a large population of Armenians reside, or from the famous Ichkhanian bakery, a must-visit in Zuqaq El Blat in Beirut and a very popular tourist spot. To my mind, these are better than cinnamon rolls. The mixture of tahini with the sugar and cinnamon creates a nice flaky pastry with sweet and savoury pockets of flavour. Delicious served with *Ashta* (page 219) or vanilla ice cream.

In a large bowl, mix the flour, salt, sugar and yeast. Make a well in the middle and pour in the water and olive oil. Bring the flour mix in and work with a wooden spoon or your hand until a shaggy dough forms. Knead until it starts to come together into a soft ball. Add more flour, if needed, but no more than a couple of tablespoons. Cover the bowl with a dish towel and set aside for 30–50 minutes until doubled in size (this will depend on the temperature of your kitchen).

Punch down the risen dough and turn out onto a lightly floured work surface. Divide into 6 pieces and shape each piece into a ball by pinching the sides down and rolling the ball in the palm of one hand against the work surface. Cover again and let rest for 15–30 minutes.

Meanwhile, preheat the oven to 200°C (400°F/gas 6).

Lightly flour each dough ball and roll into a rectangle (about 45 x 12 cm/ 18 x 5 in) with a long edge facing you. Brush a heaped tablespoon of tahini over each piece leaving a 5 mm (¼ in) border at the sides and the edge furthest away from you. Sprinkle each piece liberally with sugar and cinnamon and roll up from the edge closest to you into a long rope. Pinch the seams and roll each rope into a coil, tucking the ends underneath. Flatten with your palm or use a rolling pin to roll out each coil into a 14 cm (5½ in) round. Place on a baking sheet and let prove for a further 20 minutes.

Bake for 8–10 minutes until lightly browned. Remove and let cool.

Serve warm or at room temperature, either on their own, or with some *Ashta* (page 219) or *Ashta* Ice Cream (see page 180) for a sweet treat.

BAKERY-STYLE PITA BREAD
Khebz Aarabi

300 g (2½ cups) strong (bread) flour, plus extra for dusting

50 g (⅓ cup) wholemeal (whole-wheat) flour

1 teaspoon fine salt

1 teaspoon sugar (optional)

7 g (2 teaspoons) instant dried yeast

200 ml (scant 1 cup) warm water

olive oil, for oiling

There are several different types of bread that are traditionally made at home. *Marqouq* is a thin, crêpe-like bread baked on a dome-shaped griddle and best made with the indigenous wheat variety, *salamouni*. *Tannour* (similar to Indian *naan*) is baked inside a hot, deep, clay oven. And there's the thin commercial bread that's used to scoop most Lebanese foods off the plate. But, to me, the king of them all is the thick, round pita bread, fresh out of the oven, which is how they serve it in most Lebanese restaurants, that's steamy on the inside, chewy and thick enough to scoop up hummus or labneh. I get mine from a bakery near my house for special breakfasts of labneh, cheeses and *shakshouka*.

In a large bowl, mix the flours, salt, sugar and yeast. Make a well in the middle and pour in the water. Bring the flour mix in and work with a wooden spoon or your hands. Knead until the dough starts to come together away from the sides of the bowl. Coat the dough with a little olive oil, cover the bowl with a dish towel and set aside for 1 hour or until doubled in size.

Meanwhile, preheat the oven to 200°C (400°F/gas 6) and place a large baking sheet inside to heat up.

Punch down the risen dough and turn out onto a lightly floured work surface. Divide into 6 pieces and shape each piece into a ball by pinching the sides down and rolling the ball in the palm of one hand against the work surface. Cover again and let rest for 10 minutes.

On a lightly floured work surface, use a rolling pin to roll each ball of dough into a circle about 8 mm (³⁄₁₆ in) thick. Let rest, covered, while you roll the other balls.

Slide the breads onto the heated baking sheet and bake for 3 minutes or until puffed and browned. Alternatively, you can bake them on the stovetop in a hot dry frying pan (skillet) until they puff up, flipping them over to brown on both sides.

Eat them fresh out of the oven, or cover them with a dish towel, then store in a bag to keep them soft. Best consumed within 2–3 days; otherwise, toast or fry for fattoush or fatteh.

STREET FOOD

Being a culinary tour guide, I enjoy walking around the city streets, alleyways and staircases, introducing visitors to Beirut through bites of food, and getting to see the city through their eyes. I never get bored of the different types of *manouche* we get to try, or the fresh falafel sandwiches wrapped by the always-smiling Nader. Then there are the smoky shawarma wraps from a certain famous Lebanese restaurant, or the *kaake* from a small, dark bakery at the base of a war-torn building or from the men pulling carts piled high with the purse-shaped sesame bread through the streets of the city.

The quick option of an on-the-go meal is popular in Beirut. Wherever you are, there's bound to be a shop nearby to cater for your particular food desire. And, as the quality is consistently high, you'll rarely be disappointed. We Lebanese love our classics and restaurants do them well. Sometimes, someone will try to experiment and expand the range of options or flavours available, but we are purists at heart (have you seen a Lebanese getting furious about the wrong *tabbouleh*!?). We are prepared to accept things that are truly different and new, but not poorly altered versions of our beloved originals! In this chapter I give you a taste of some of the best – and most classic – on-the-go food the city has to offer.

TOPPED LEBANESE FLATBREADS
Manouche

What came first: pizza or *manouche*? Of course, we'd say *manouche*, and back it up with facts (real or made up, it doesn't matter) about how it came from our region. A *manouche* (plural: *manaeesh*) is a round flatbread, traditionally topped with za'atar or white cheese. The name comes from the Arabic *na'esh*, which means 'to engrave', as you punch your fingers into the dough to prevent it puffing up into pita bread. It really is the king of breakfasts. Many is the time I grab a za'atar *manouche* wrapped around some fresh veggies from the local baker on my way to work. On other, slower, days, we'll have a dozen with mixed toppings for a home breakfast served with green olives, pickles, fresh mint, tomatoes, cucumbers and a warm cup of tea flavoured with rose geranium leaves.

This recipe makes soft, round *manouche*, but you can roll the dough thinner for a crispier version, although you'll need more topping.

In a large bowl, combine the flour with the salt, sugar and yeast. Make a well in the middle, add the water and olive oil and mix with a wooden spoon or your hands. Knead until the dough comes together away from the sides of the bowl. Coat the ball of dough with a little oil, cover the bowl with a dish towel and leave to prove in a warm place for 1 hour or until doubled in size.

Meanwhile, preheat the oven to 200°C (400°F/gas 6) and place a baking sheet in the oven to heat up.

Punch down the risen dough and and turn out onto a lightly floured work surface. Divide into 6 pieces and shape each piece into a ball by pinching the sides down and rolling in the palm of one hand against the work surface. Cover again and let rest for 10 minutes. Lightly flour the surface and rolling pin, then roll the dough balls into circles 8–10 mm (¾ in) thick. Cover and leave to rest for a further 10 minutes.

Poke the rounds with a fork or dimple with your fingers to prevent them from puffing up, then top each with your favourite topping (see page 49). Bake on the hot baking sheet for about 8 minutes (or as stated, depending on the topping) until the dough is lightly browned and the toppings are cooked through. Serve warm.

350 g (2¾ cups) strong (bread) flour, plus extra for dusting

1 teaspoon fine salt

1 teaspoon white caster (superfine) sugar or honey (optional)

7 g (2 teaspoons) instant dried yeast

200 ml (scant 1 cup) warm water

60 ml (¼ cup) olive oil, plus extra for coating

Toppings
see page 49

To serve
pickles, fresh sliced vegetables and olives

KISHK TOPPING

MAKES ENOUGH FOR 2 *MANOUCHE*

100 g (3½ oz) onions, finely chopped

100 g (3½ oz) dried kishk (a.k.a. kashk – a fermented yoghurt product that you can find in Middle Eastern shops or online)

1½ tablespoons tomato paste (concentrated purée)

1½ teaspoons chilli powder

1½ tablespoons sesame seeds, plus extra for sprinkling

60 ml (¼ cup) olive oil

60 ml (¼ cup) water, or as needed

Place all the ingredients in a bowl and mix to combine, adding enough water to hydrate the *kishk* until you have a thick paste.

Poke the *manouche* dough rounds with a fork or dimple with your fingers to prevent it rising. Spread the *kishk* topping over the top of each round and bake for 8-10 minutes until the dough is lightly browned and the *kishk* is cooked through.

Sprinkle with more sesame seeds before serving, if you like.

Note: Shredded mozzarella or Akkawi cheese (or a mix of mozzarella and ricotta cheese, if you can't get Akkawi) can be mixed in with the *kishk* paste to make it extra cheesy. The chilli powder can also be replaced with chilli paste or chopped fresh chillies to increase the heat.

ZA'ATAR ON ZA'ATAR TOPPING

MAKES ENOUGH FOR 2 *MANOUCHE*

80 g (scant ⅓ cup) tomato paste (concentrated purée)

2 tablespoons sumac

60 ml (¼ cup) olive oil

1 bunch of fresh wild thyme, leaves picked (preferably the one with the long thin leaves, *see note*)

2 tablespoons sesame seeds

In a bowl, mix the tomato paste and sumac with 2 tablespoons of the olive oil until well combined.

Poke the *manouche* dough rounds with a fork or dimple with your fingers to prevent it rising. Spread the topping mixture over the top of each round and bake for 8 minutes until the dough is lightly browned.

Generously top with the picked thyme leaves and sesame seeds and drizzle with the remaining olive oil before serving.

Note: If wild thyme is diffficult to find, try adding baby rocket (arugula) leaves and flavour with some fresh marjoram, regular thyme or dried thyme.

BEIRUTI-STYLE MEAT CIGARS
Lahm Baajine Beiruti

175 ml (¾ cup) olive oil

60 g (⅔ cup) flaked (slivered) almonds or pine nuts

250 g (9 oz) onions, finely chopped

400 g (14 oz) minced (ground) beef

2 teaspoons salt

2 tablespoons ground cinnamon

2 teaspoons allspice

½ teaspoon ground nutmeg

½ teaspoon ground cloves

10 filo (phyllo) pastry sheets (about 30 x 20 cm/12 x 8 in)

To serve (optional)
pomegranate molasses, for drizzling
thick plain yoghurt, for dipping
Ayran (page 199), to drink

Lahm baajine is another *manouche* topping, but usually served on a cracker-thin dough that barely carries the meat topping (see top left image on page 53). Beiruti-style *lahm baajine* are made from a thin dough, lifted and repeatedly slapped on an oiled surface until it is see-through. This version is rarely available around town nowadays – only in specific places – but you'll surely find it at almost every corner in old Saida (the local name for the city of Sidon to the south of Beirut).

I thought I'd skip the dough-making and make sure you get it right by using filo pastry sheets. Brushing the sheets with oil will make them so crispy when baked.

Heat 2 tablespoons of the olive oil in a large frying pan (skillet) over a medium heat and fry the almonds or pine nuts until golden. Remove with a slotted spoon to drain on paper towels. Add the onions to the pan and cook until translucent, then add the beef, salt and all the spices. Cook, stirring to break up the beef, until well browned. Stir the almonds or pine nuts back in, then remove the pan from the heat and let cool.

Meanwhile, preheat the oven to 200°C (400°F/gas 6) and grease a baking sheet with olive oil.

To assemble, lay a filo pastry sheet on your work surface and cut it in half lengthways. Arrange a couple of tablespoons of the filling mixture in a line on the part of the pastry closest to you, leaving a 1 cm (½ in) margin around it on 3 edges. Fold in the edges and roll over to enclose the filling, creating a cigar-shaped parcel. Brush the remainder of the sheet with oil and keep rolling until the roll is complete. Place on the prepared baking sheet and repeat until all the pastry sheets and filling mixture are used up.

Generously brush the pastries with any remaining olive oil and bake for 10–13 minutes or until golden.

Serve immediately to preserve that desirable crunch from the layers of pastry. These taste good with a drizzle of pomegranate molasses and some thick yoghurt for dipping, perhaps with a glass of *ayran* on the side.

SFEEHA

Wherever you go throughout Lebanon, each area has a different version of sfeeha – the traditional combination of meat and dough. From *Lahm Baajine* to the *Sfeeha* or *Sambousek*, the names signify a different type in each region.

In Beirut, *Lahm Baajine* is usually a cracker-thin *manouche* topped with a meat mixture. Lebanese style is to top them with beef, with tomatoes, onions and certain spices. Armenian bakeries serve one with pomegranate molasses that is so warm and sweet and another with parsley, onions and tomatoes that has more of a savoury taste. The Beiruti style is more like a thin, oiled dough wrapping a cooked filling (see the recipe on page 51) that turns into a delicious crispy snack when baked. In general, a Beiruti *Sfeeha* is a small square of pastry pinched at the four corners to hold a filling of yoghurt and spiced marinated meat.

In Tripoli, North Lebanon, *Sfeeha* is a thick pita bread filled with a meat mixture and baked, similar to *Arayes Kafta* (page 54) only with different spices,

while *Lahm Baajine* is layers of puff pastry topped with a sweet and savoury pomegranate molasses and meat mixture. Baalbak, in eastern Lebanon, is known for its *Sfeeha* (*Sfeeha Baalbakiye*), which are the same shape as the common Sfeeha with a delicious, fatty, spiced lamb filling with no yoghurt. You can't, and shouldn't, go to Baalbak without having one. In Saida (Sidon), southern Lebanon, in the tiny, pedestrianised streets of the old city, you'll find a baker who makes a great *Lahm Baajine* similar to the Beirut style. Thin and crispy parcels envelop a warm, spiced, cooked meat filling.

The one that there is less fuss about is the *Sambousek* – a thin pastry that's usually fried stuffed with a cooked meat filling. They can also be baked, but you'd be missing out on the incredible crunch and the tiny little bubbles that rise to the surface from the yeasted dough.

Whatever choice you make and whichever Lebanese city you're visiting, you are certain to be rewarded with wonderful treats along the way.

KOFTA IN PITA BREAD SANDWICHES
Arayes Kafta

This is another of the many meat and bread recipes that abound in Lebanon. The meat options are plentiful, and so are the dough or bread varieties. This one is a home-style replica of *kafta bil aajine*, a grab-and-go item often seen in Lebanese fast-food chains and a popular post-drinking food after a night out in the bars and clubs.

For my home-made version, you can follow the *Manouche* recipe on page 46 and top the punched-down dough with the meat filling and bake it, or bake some extra loaves to fill and bake again, or use store-bought pita bread.

Although it's not traditional, it is a popular custom among the young crowd of Beirut to top *arayes* with mayo. I'd suggest a good slather of *Toom* garlic sauce (pages 68–71) or a good chilli paste are also amazing fiery serving options.

In a large bowl, mix together the beef, onions, parsley, allspice and salt until well combined.

Open the pita breads and fill with the beef mixture. Toast on a panini press (or in a dry hot pan with a weight on top, turning once) until well browned and the meat is cooked through.

Alternatively, place on a lined baking sheet and bake in the oven at 190°C (375°F/gas 5) for 7–10 minutes, turning once, until browned and the meat is cooked through.

Serve with some chilli sauce for dipping or with a drizzle of mayo, as is trendy around Beirut, with a refreshing yoghurt salad or *ayran*, the local yoghurt drink, on the side.

600 g (1 lb 5 oz) coarsely minced (ground) beef (10% fat)

80 g (3 oz) onions, finely chopped

handful of flat-leaf parsley, finely chopped

½ teaspoon allspice

1 teaspoon sea salt

3 large or 4 small pita breads (store-bought or home-made, page 39) or home-made *manouche* (*see introduction*)

To serve

chilli sauce (red pepper paste) of choice, for dipping

mayo, for drizzling

Cucumber and Yoghurt Salad (page 81)

Ayran (page 199), to drink

LEBANESE STREET BREAD
Ka'ak Asrouniye

MAKES 6

A trip down memory lane. Every afternoon – after the post-lunch nap and before the light started to fade – a delightful, piercing honk would cut through the shouts of kids playing in the streets. A guy on a motorcycle, with a skeletal box covered in thick plastic sheeting set behind him, would announce his arrival with a few honks on an old-fashioned horn, like the ones clowns use. The older generation here remember the man who held a wooden tray on his head, balanced with a special cushion and excellent core strength, and a foldable table that he carried around to make any place his marketplace with just a couple of honks on the horn. People would go down from their homes to buy *ka'ak asrouniye*, filled with a sprinkle of za'atar or sumac, or filled with soft spreadable cheese, to nibble on with their coffee or tea.

Ka'ak (not to be confused with sweet *kaak*, which are the crunchy sesame and mahlab breadsticks or cookies traditionally served with hot drinks) is a traditional Levantine sesame bread, like a thick pita, crunchy on the outside and soft and pillowy on the inside. Vendors roam the streets with carts loaded with different types of *ka'ak*, usually as purse-shaped breads with a handle. In Tripoli, in North Lebanon, the *kaaké* (singular) is shaped into a circle with no holes, baked and filled with Akkawi cheese, then grilled in small shacks or on carts anywhere in the souk.

In this recipe, the sesame coating is mixed with molasses – a tip I learned from one of the oldest family bakeries on the port-side of Tripoli – which gives the *kaaké* a good brown colour and that distinctive flavour.

In a large bowl, combine the flours and add the salt, sugar and yeast. Make a well in the middle, pour in the water and mix with a wooden spoon or your hands. Knead until the dough comes together away from the sides of the bowl, then turn out onto the work surface and knead for 5 minutes until you get a nice smooth dough. Coat in olive oil, place in a bowl, cover, and prove for 1 hour or until doubled in size.

Preheat the oven to 200°C (400°F/gas 6).

Punch down the dough and divide into 6 pieces, then shape into balls. Cover and rest for a further 10 minutes.

300 g (2½ cups) white strong (bread) flour

150 g (1 cup) wholemeal (whole-wheat) flour

2 teaspoons fine salt

1 tablespoon sugar

10 g (1 tablespoon) instant dried yeast

250 ml (1 cup) water

olive oil, for drizzling

For the coating

1 teaspoon carob molasses

2 teaspoons warm water

30 g (¼ cup) untoasted sesame seeds

To serve

olive oil, for drizzling

za'atar (optional)

sumac (optional)

recipe continues overleaf...›

...> Meanwhile, make the coating. Dilute the molasses with the warm water and mix with the sesame seeds.

Dip each ball of dough into the coating on both sides (or stick to just one side if it's tough to roll). Roll each out with a rolling pin to 1 cm (½ in) thick. If you prefer, you can form them into the traditional purse shapes, but it's not essential.

Line a baking sheet with baking paper. Transfer the shaped breads to the baking sheet and leave to rest for 10 minutes.

Bake for 5–7 minutes until browned and slightly puffed. Remove from the oven and cover with a dish towel to keep them soft.

To serve, slice the breads at the seam and fill with a drizzle of olive oil and a good za'atar mix or with sumac, as is traditional. Alternatively, fill with sliced white cheese (see right) and grill (broil). Serve with a tray of fresh vegetables, mint, olives and cups of tea.

SPICY CHEESE KA'AK

During Ramadan, particularly in Tripoli, it is a common *sohour* practice to walk to the bakery and ask for several pieces of *ka'ak*, then cross to the cheese vendor across the street, select your favourite combinations, and return to the bakery for the baker to slice the buns open, stuff them with the cheeses and heat them in the ovens until the cheese melts.

SERVES 2

1 Lebanese *Ka'ak* (page 56), warmed

1 tablespoon chilli paste (use your favourite store-bought paste)

2 tablespoons olive oil

100 g (3½ oz) soft mild goat's cheese or White Baladi Goat's Cheese (page 218)

50 g (2 oz) mozzarella, shredded

vegetable sticks and fresh mint, to serve

Preheat the oven to 160°C (320°F/gas 2).

While the *ka'ak* is soft and warm, take a knife and cut into it at the seam to form a pocket.

Stir together the chilli paste and olive oil until you have a homogeneous mixture. Spread this over the upper inside of the pocket in the *ka'ak*. On the other side, crumble the white cheese and spread the mozzarella on top.

Put the *ka'ak* on a baking sheet and bake for 10–15 minutes until the cheese has melted.

Cut the *ka'ak* into 4 pieces and serve with some vegetables and fresh mint.

SPINACH PIES
Fatayer Sbenekh

There are endless varieties of Lebanese pastries and each type itself varies to the extent of minute differences in herbs to vegetables, cultivated or foraged. *Fatayer* means 'pies', which colloquially means a closed, stuffed hand-pastry; the filling name comes as a suffix (in Arabic). The home-style version of these pastries are small, one- or two-bite-sized, and served alongside a soup, as my mom usually does in winter, or as part of a *meza* spread preceding a main dish. Bakeries around the country now serve palm-sized versions for hungry people picking up a quick breakfast or lunch option.

What really makes this recipe worth trying is the combination of sumac and olive oil in the filling – it has a tangy kick with the mellow spinach. I add a squeeze of lemon before taking a bite, as it enhances the flavour and helps the body absorb iron from the spinach.

Start with the filling. Chop the spinach into thick ribbons and rub with the rock salt. Place in a colander in the sink and leave for 30 minutes–1 hour to drain. At the end of this time, squeeze out as much liquid as you can, then place the spinach in a bowl and set aside.

Rub the onions with the sumac and add them to the spinach, then add the lemon juice, citric acid, chilli paste and olive oil, stir to combine and leave to marinate for 2 hours, or overnight in the refrigerator.

To make the dough, mix the flour, salt and sugar with the olive oil in a bowl, rubbing the oil into the flour until it has a coarse sandy texture. Add the water a little at a time, mixing with your hands until the dough comes together. Cover with a dish towel and let it rest for 30 minutes.

Meanwhile, preheat the oven to 200°C (400°F/gas 6).

When the filling is ready, drain off any excess liquid. Take a piece of the dough and roll out on an oiled work surface to about 3 mm (1/8 in) thick, or as thinly as possible. Cut into 11 cm (4½ in) circles using a cookie cutter or a glass.

Fill the middle of each circle of dough with a little of the filling, brush the edge of the circle with a little water, then pinch half of the circle together

For the filling

1 kg (2 lb 4 oz) fresh spinach, washed and dried

2 teaspoons rock salt

250 g (9 oz) onions, very finely chopped

1 tablespoon sumac

1 tablespoon freshly squeezed lemon juice

½ teaspoon citric acid

1 teaspoon chilli paste

scant 3 tablespoons olive oil

For the dough

300 g (2½ cups) plain (all-purpose) flour

1 teaspoon fine salt

3 teaspoons sugar

60 ml (¼ cup) olive oil, plus extra for oiling and brushing

100 ml (scant ½ cup) water

to close. Lift up the unclosed edge of the circle and pinch it together with the adjacent unclosed edges (to create a sort of pyramid shape with the seams). Adjust the filling portions as you go based on how easy it is to close the parcels without having the filling ooze out. Generously brush the pastries with olive oil and place on a baking sheet.

Bake for 12–15 minutes or until golden brown on the top and bottom. Let cool slightly before serving.

Note: The unbaked pastries can be frozen in a single layer on a baking sheet until solid, then stored in a bag to bake when needed. Bake at 200°C (400°F/gas 6) for 15–20 minutes until golden.

FALAFEL
Falefil

When I ask foreign visitors what Lebanese food they've had before, one of the first things they'll say is falafel. Falafel shops are scattered around the country, and each region has its own favourite, but the most notable falafel shops in Beirut are those of 'the feuding brothers', Sahyoun. These two identically named shops, each owned by an estranged brother and each vying for the title of 'best falafel in Beirut', are found on Damascus Street, or what I like to call Falafel Street. The street connects Sodeco Square to Martyrs' Square and was the former Green Line of the civil war that separated Beirut into East and West. On that street, a few shops before the feuding brothers' outlets, is the maker of *my* favourite falafel: Aboulziz. The falafel balls never last long there – they are never left to become cold, sad balls – but are always prepared and fried in small batches to keep them fresh. The man knows me and greets me and my guests with a piece drizzled with *tarator* (tahini sauce) to keep us munching as he rolls the generously filled falafel sandwiches. Here, that means a wrap – not a sliced pita bread that's strangely stuffed with ingredients where you can't get a bit of everything in each bite.

When building your own wrap, don't skip on the mint and parsley, as they brighten the flavour, or the chillies, if you're into a bit of heat. The acidity of the fermented turnip matches the falafel perfectly, but you can replace it with cucumber pickles (no dill, for me, here) or the wild/Armenian cucumber pickle, which is my favourite.

Using tinned or pre-boiled chickpeas (garbanzo beans) will result in a mushier consistency, which explains why some recipes add flour to bind the ingredients together. It is much better to soak your own beans and grind and mix them uncooked. They will cook to perfection in the oil.

Soak the dried chickpeas and beans overnight in plenty of water.

The next day, drain the soaked beans and put both into a food processor along with the onions and garlic. Pulse intermittently until you have small granules – not too fine, otherwise the falafel will be dense.

400 g (scant 2 cups) dried chickpeas (garbanzo beans)

200 g (1¼ cups) dried split broad (fava) beans

250 g (9 oz) onions (2 small onions), roughly chopped

30 g (1 oz) garlic (7–8 cloves)

1 tablespoon salt

3 tablespoons ground cumin

3 tablespoons ground caraway

4 tablespoons ground coriander

2 tablespoons garlic powder

1 tablespoon baking powder

2 tablespoons cornflour (cornstarch)

vegetable oil, for deep-frying

For the tahini sauce
275 g (1 cup) tahini

175 ml (¾ cup) cold water

175 ml (¾ cup) freshly squeezed lemon juice

½ teaspoon salt

To serve
pickled turnips

pickled chillies

mint leaves

flat-leaf parsley leaves

sliced tomatoes

thin flatbread wraps or pita bread

Transfer the mixture to a bowl and mix in the salt, spices, baking powder and cornflour until well combined.

Pour enough vegetable oil for deep-frying into a deep, heavy-based pan and heat over a medium heat to 160°C (320°F) or until a cube of bread dropped into the oil browns in 40 seconds.

Shape small balls from the falafel mixture using a traditional falafel scoop or an ice-cream scoop. Don't press the mix too firmly, otherwise the falafel will be dense. Lower them into the hot oil and deep-fry for 2–3 minutes, flipping as needed, until golden brown on both sides. You may need to do this in batches. Remove with a slotted spoon to drain on paper towels.

For the tahini sauce, mix the tahini with the cold water until smooth – the mixture will separate at first, but will come together again. Season with lemon juice and salt to taste.

Serve the hot falafel with the tahini sauce, with pickled turnips and chillies, mint, parsley, tomatoes and pita bread on the side.

STREET FOOD

CHICKEN SHAWARMA
Shawerma Djej

Shawarma has gained massive international popularity in the past few years (is it because of the last scene in one of the *Avengers* movies or because of how well it's made!?). Its popularity never faded here, but it had a resurgence with restaurants trying new twists and mostly failing to impress an audience used to a certain combination – even me, usually a rather adventurous eater. The classic shawarma is still the clear winner.

It being a quick pick-me-up street food, I wouldn't normally go to a restaurant and order a shawarma sandwich as a dine-in guest. However, at Boubouffe, a restaurant in the Achrafieh district, which grills the shawarma spits over real charcoal, as opposed to electric or gas vertical grills, it is worth trying. The smoky flavour that the charcoal imparts really complements the marinating spices.

The texture and flavours of that shawarma are not easy to replicate, even with the new gadgets available to roast mini shawarma spits at home, as they overcook the outer layer of chicken to be able to properly cook the inside, and that compromises the moisture in the meat. The mastery of restaurant-made shawarma is in the perfect seasoning and marination; in properly and slowly cooking the meat by exposing all sides to heat; shaving off the sides with excellent knife skills; the sandwiches get that final juicy kick when the shaved meat is briefly tossed in the precious fat drippings underneath the spit. This recipe tries to come close to that experience, but I had to ask a master for help – my dad. Always have it with extra *toom*!

In a dry, hot pan, toast the cardamom, bay leaves, white peppercorns and coriander seeds until fragrant. Transfer to a spice grinder or a pestle and mortar and grind to a powder, then set aside.

In a large bowl, combine the chicken strips with the onions, oil, vinegar, salt, nutmeg and the spice powder. Cover with cling film (plastic wrap) and marinate overnight in the refrigerator.

2 cardamom pods

5 bay leaves

1 tablespoon white peppercorns

1 tablespoon coriander seeds

1 kg (2 lb 4 oz) skinless chicken (breast or thigh), sliced into thin strips

400 g (14 oz) onions, thinly sliced

120 ml (½ cup) olive oil

120 ml (½ cup) white vinegar

2 teaspoons salt

1 teaspoon ground nutmeg

For the *toom* garlic sauce

100 g (3½ oz) garlic cloves

300 ml (1¼ cups) vegetable oil

2 teaspoons sea salt

2 tablespoons freshly squeezed lemon juice

For the sandwich

6 pita breads

6 cucumber (or wild cucumber) pickles, sliced

a handful of cooked French fries or chips

1 head romaine lettuce (6–7 leaves)

recipe continues overleaf...›

...› For the *toom* garlic sauce, prepare by placing the peeled garlic in the refrigerator overnight. Measure out the oil and place in a jar in the freezer. This is a foolproof method to get a good *toom*, since it keeps the temperature of the paste low while grinding and prevents separating.

The next day, preheat the oven to 200°C (400°F/gas 6).

Drain most of the liquid from the marinated chicken and onions and spread the mixture over a baking sheet in an even layer.

Bake for 20 minutes, then remove and toss the mixture with a spatula and spread it out again. Return to the oven for a further 20 minutes until the edges of the chicken are starting to get crispy.

Meanwhile, finish making the toom garlic sauce. Blitz the chilled garlic cloves in a food processor to a paste. With the motor still running, drizzle in the cold oil through the feed tube very slowly until it is fully incorporated. Make sure to stop and scrape down the sides from time to time until a thick, creamy sauce is formed. Add the salt and lemon juice to taste, and thin out with a little water if necessary, mixing until you reach your desired consistency.

To assemble the sandwich, spread some *toom* inside a pita bread, top it with the chicken shawarma, and add some pickles, French fries and some lettuce. For an extra crunch, grill (broil) the wrap, seam down, until slightly browned and serve.

Note: Any unsued *toom* can be stored in an airtight container in the refrigerator for up to 5 days. In addition to being great with this sandwich, you can use it as a marinade or a side for grilled (broiled) chicken; mix it with labneh; slather it on top of good sliced heirloom tomatoes with sumac and flaky salt; or just be creative!

ARMENIAN SPICY SAUSAGES
Soujok

800 g (2 lb 4 oz) finely minced (ground) beef (20% fat)

3 garlic cloves, minced

3 tablespoons red pepper paste

For the Soujok Spice Mix

½ teaspoon allspice

1½ teaspoons white pepper

1 teaspoon black pepper

1 tablespoon ground cumin

2 teaspoons salt

¼ teaspoon ground nutmeg

1½ tablespoons garlic powder

1½ tablespoons paprika

1½ tablespoons dried chilli (red pepper) flakes

1½ tablespoons ground fenugreek

To serve

hotdog buns, split

tomatoes, sliced

gherkins or wild cucumber pickles, sliced

Armenians expelled from their homeland over a hundred years ago took refuge in the Levant, between Syria (mainly Aleppo), Lebanon and Palestine. While they preserved their culture and language, they started to merge their cooking with the produce from the lands they settled in. This cultural marriage created the Aleppo-Armenian style of cooking that in Lebanon we know as Armenian food.

Bourj Hammoud is one of the neighbourhoods on the outskirts of Greater Beirut and home to a large Armenian population. There's a small shop there called Mano that makes the most popular Armenian cured meat products: *soujok* (a large spicy sausage), *maqaneq* (small sausages flavoured with warm spices and pine nuts) and *basterma* (spiced air-dried cured meat). I've loved it since I used to visit with my aunt when I was about fourteen and it was always one of the places to stop at to grab the best *soujok* sandwiches, along with its nearby rival, Bedo.

Prepare this recipe by mixing the meat with the spices and leaving it in the refrigerator, covered, to marinate – the longer the better for the best flavour. Use the sausages for these hot-dog-style sandwiches or serve with French fries, fried eggs or roasted vegetables.

In a large bowl, combine the beef, garlic, red pepper paste and spice mix and work with your hands until it is well combined. Leave to marinate in the refrigerator for a few hours, or ideally overnight, even up to 36 hours, to develop the flavour.

Shape the soujok mixture into 10 cm (4 in) sausages.

Heat a splash of olive oil in a shallow frying pan (skillet) over a medium–high heat. Fry the sausages until browned on all sides and cooked through.

To serve, lightly grill (broil) the hotdogs buns on a grill pan, so that they have some lovely grill marks on them. Fill the buns with the cooked soujok and slices of tomatoes and pickles.

Note: You can eat them just like this, but I also like to serve them as toasted sandwiches, toasting them in a panini press or in a dry pan with a weight on top.

SALADS
& SIDES

In Lebanon, we are not short on produce. Our location provides us with an ideal environment to grow everything from simple herbs and greens, to citrus fruits, avocados, apples, cherries and other stone fruits, even wine-grade grapes. Alongside farmed produce, the hillsides are filled with wild edible greens that people have found ways to process and make delicious. Cooks of old found ways to utilise everything grown on the land or forageable, be it sautéing, preserving in oil, fermenting in salt brine, or quick-curing with oil and salt for a refreshing salad. I could go a hundred days alone just on local produce, getting more creative every time. Our Mediterranean cuisine is loaded with vegan dishes, many of them can have meat or chicken added to them, but they're good on their own.

There are salads aplenty in our home-cooking repertoire, but two race to the top: *tabbouleh* and *fattoush*. I am more of a 'team *tabbouleh*' person on almost any day. A delicious way to pump up a leftover *tabbouleh*, where the burghul has soaked up so much liquid and the veggies have become a little too wet or soggy, is to mix in cooked and cooled freekeh or lentils. A grilled and sliced chicken breast can also make it more filling. Restaurants repurpose leftover *tabbouleh* into the famous vegetarian vine leaf rolls by adding rice and chickpeas (garbanzo beans) for a no-waste stuffing.

And, of course, the table is never complete without the perfect side dishes. Our olives, firm and sharp, are delicious straight out of the jar, and there are always zesty salads and crunchy pickles. Even in the most economically challenging times, families will switch up foods for affordable options but still maintain a properly spread table. Recently, due to the catastrophic events of 2020, lots of families were forced to slow down and start changing their habits and learning new ones. I've noticed people asking for advice on ways to cook and preserve foods they were never interested in before. Foraged greens, balcony potted herbs, pickles, fruit rinds and skins. There's always a way to use everything. In fact, lots of our traditional dishes were born out of necessity and threats of food shortages. Our large selection of *mouneh* (preserves) were born out of those two concepts: you store the excess you have for the toughest days, be they due to the weather, hardships of war or economic and political instability.

TABBOULEH

We couldn't call this a classic Levantine cookbook without a *tabbouleh* recipe! If I want to determine how authentic the recipes in a Lebanese cookbook are, the first thing I look at is the recipe for *tabbouleh*. I am ultra-judgmental about it – if the ratio of parsley to any other ingredient is too low, I don't trust the book.

The origin of *tabbouleh* predates the creation of the current borders in the Levant. Therefore, to me, a country claiming ownership of the dish is absurd, especially when there are so many regional variations. Some use mint; others would not eat a *tabbouleh* with mint in it. Cucumbers and shredded lettuce are also regional additions. But the most suprising I ever heard of was the recipe described to me by some Brazilian siblings of Lebanese descent: their grandma's *tabbouleh* recipe, that she had carried with her and prepared in the same way as she had when she was a young girl in the Lebanon, was a main meal with lots of bulgur and very little parsley or tomatoes. It's really up to you to make it the way you like it, but this is the version you're most likely to find on Lebanese menus.

Chop the herbs. The trick to properly chop herbs is to have a really sharp knife. Tightly bunch up the parsley, then chop off the stems (keep them in a freezer bag for stocks and soups). Start moving your knife down the parsley leaves with a firm chopping motion in very close strokes. Don't go over it a second time, as the leaves will bruise and darken and lose their freshness. Repeat for the mint, if using.

Finely chop the tomatoes into the smallest dice you can and thinly slice the spring onions. If you're using regular onions, finely dice them the smallest you can and rub them with salt and allspice to soften their punch (this also prevents them turning rancid if prepared ahead of time).

Add all the ingredients to a large bowl. Toss with two spoons, or use your hands to do it the authentic way. Taste and adjust the seasonings as you wish. Serve with lettuce leaves or young and tender vine leaves, when in season, for scooping.

150 g (5 oz) flat-leaf parsley, washed and dried

leaves from 3 large sprigs of fresh mint (optional)

400 g (14 oz) tomatoes

70 g (2½ oz) spring onions (scallions) or 30 g (1 oz) brown onions

2 tablespoons fine uncooked bulgur wheat

zest of 1 lemon

120 ml (½ cup) freshly squeezed lemon juice (or verjuice)

120 ml (½ cup) olive oil

¼ teaspoon allspice, or to taste

1 teaspoon salt, or to taste

lettuce leaves or young vine leaves, to serve

FATTOUSH

If you are not Team *Tabbouleh*, then you are Team *Fattoush*. These two are the top salads you'll find in any restaurant serving Lebanese food. *Fattoush* can actually be a fridge clean-up salad – you can basically toss in whatever fresh veggies and leafy greens you have to hand, but the unchangeable elements, for me, are the purslane and the sumac dressing. Restaurants use lettuce as a base because it's cheaper and easier to deal with, and pomegranate molasses instead of sumac because it can be found cheaper. But I find that the tang and slight bitterness of sumac is irreplaceable.

My favourite way of serving this dish – the best and only way! – is with the fried bread on the side of the dressed salad. I break off two small pieces of bread and use them to scoop up a mouthful of the salad ingredients. Don't be afraid to get messy and lick your fingers afterwards.

Cut the bread into triangles and toss in a bowl with 2 tablespoons of the olive oil and 1 tablespoon of the sumac. Toast under a hot grill (broiler) or in a hot, dry pan (or fry in a little vegetable oil, if wished), until golden and crispy. If frying, you can skip adding the sumac. Set aside to cool and drain on paper towels.

In a large bowl, mix together the salad leaves, herbs, radishes, tomatoes, cucumbers and onions. If using red onions, rub them with 1 tablespoon of sumac.

Dress the salad with the remaining olive oil, lemon juice and salt, and toss to combine.

Top with the crispy bread and serve immediately.

2 pita breads

120 ml (½ cup) olive oil

1–2 tablespoons sumac

100 g (3½ oz) purslane, lettuce or leafy green (leaves and tender stems only)

handful of fresh thyme leaves (about 20 g/¾ oz)

handful of fresh mint leaves (about 20 g/¾ oz)

4–5 radishes, thinly sliced

350 g (10½ oz) tomatoes, roughly chopped

200 g (7 oz) Lebanese cucumbers, sliced and cut into half moons

3–4 spring onions (scallions) or ½ red onion, thinly sliced

120 ml (½ cup) freshly squeezed lemon juice

½ teaspoon sea salt

ROCKET SALAD
Salatet Rocca

200 g (7 oz) rocket (arugula) leaves, roughly chopped

a few sprigs of wild thyme (10 g/½ oz), leaves roughly chopped (optional)

1 medium red onion, thinly sliced

1 tablespoon sumac

½ teaspoon sea salt

120 ml (½ cup) lemon juice, or to taste

60 ml (¼ cup) extra virgin olive oil, or to taste

Another restaurant classic, this salad acquires a nice zing from the sumac and the bitterness of the rocket (arugula) leaves. Feel free to try it with other bitter or wild leafy greens, such as chicory, or an assortment including wild mustard greens and blossoms. You can prepare the onions ahead of time to soften and lose a bit of their sharpness, but the salad should be assembled only just before serving, otherwise the greens will wilt. This salad also benefits from using good quality extra virgin olive oil to enhance the 'green' taste and round out the slightly bitter flavours.

Place the rocket and thyme, if using, in a bowl.

In a separate bowl, rub the sliced onion with the sumac and salt, then add to the salad and mix well.

Add the lemon juice and olive oil, adjusting to taste, and toss to combine. Serve immediately.

SERVES 4

CUCUMBER & YOGHURT SALAD
Laban w Khyar

200 g (7 oz) Lebanese cucumbers, finely chopped, or 300g/10½ oz regular cucumbers, deseeded and finely chopped

1 small garlic clove, crushed (optional)

1 teaspoon dried mint (see note on page 82)

500 g (2 cups) plain yoghurt

sea salt, to taste

This is one of the easiest and most versatile side dishes you can make. Elevate it by making your own yoghurt (see page 216). The yoghurt we have here in the Lebanon is thick and creamy, with a rich and tangy flavour. It is different to Greek yoghurt, which is much thicker. This is delicious served with *kibbeh*, either the meat or pumpkin versions (pages 113 and 156), any freekeh or rice pilaf, *Mjaddara* (page 137), *Lahm Baajine* (page 51), or just on its own as a simple snack.

Place the chopped cucumbers in a bowl. Add the garlic, if using, along with the dried mint and the yoghurt. Mix well, then season to taste with salt and serve.

ZESTY CABBAGE SALAD
Salatet Malfouf maa' Bou Sfeir

There are a few dishes I can't imagine without this salad on the side; two of them are in this book (*Mjaddara* on page 137 and *Kibbeh Bil Sayniye* on page 113) and I hope you get to associate them like I do. This salad always reminds me of darker winter days when cabbages and bitter oranges have just come into season. If you can't get bitter orange juice, use fresh lemon juice to season this instead.

Place the sliced cabbage in a large bowl.

If using fresh mint leaves, roll the leaves into a tight roll and thinly slice into ribbons, then add to the cabbage bowl. If using dried mint, simply add straight to the bowl.

Pound the garlic and salt together in a pestle and mortar to a rough paste (or just use a garlic crusher and mix the salt into the garlic paste). Add the bitter orange or lemon juice and olive oil and mix to combine.

Pour the dressing over the cabbage mixture and toss to combine. Taste and adjust the seasoning as you wish.

Note: To make your own dried mint, simply pick the fresh leaves from their sprigs and spread over a baking sheet. Toast in an oven set to its lowest setting for about 5–10 minutes until the leaves are dry but still green. Alternatively, you can spread any extra mint you have over a baking sheet or tray and leave in a dry spot away from direct sunlight for a few days, checking every now and then to ensure no wet spots or mould are forming, until completely dry. Coarsely grind in a pestle and mortar and store in a jar for later.

500 g (1 lb 2 oz) white cabbage, thinly sliced

large handful of fresh mint leaves or 1 teaspoon dried mint (see note)

2 garlic cloves

½ teaspoon salt, or more to taste

150 ml (⅔ cup) bitter orange juice (or 120 ml/½ cup lemon juice), to taste

60 ml (¼ cup) olive oil

WILD PLANTS, PRESERVES & FARMERS' MARKETS

As a nature enthusiast, I've picked up a few things about the wild foods that grow on our hillsides. A short walk away from where I grew up, my mom and grandma used to take my sister and me foraging up the steep hills on early spring days when the sun was out and the sky was clear. We used to look in the green and yellow blossoming fields for things like *a'akoub*, a thorny shoot prized for the flesh inside its bud. We'd carefully pull them out of the ground, trying not to get pricked, and clip off the leaves to reach the inner bulbs, which would be cooked with yoghurt or fried with eggs or meat. They are highly prized by those who know their flavour. We also looked for *ors a'anné* (*Eryngium creticum*), whose glossy leaves grow almost flat to the ground. We'd pick them by slicing right above the root. The raw leaves are edible when very young and tender and their peppery taste hasn't yet become sharp. Once they're

tougher, they're good in salads, mellowed by olive oil, lemon and salt. They also make a good filling for *fatayer* and are perfect for sautéing with onions and eating with bread and a squeeze of lemon juice, as are most foraged greens. Later in the season, this plant grows tall and thorny and is no longer edible. We'd also look for sage, sorrel, wild thyme and wild rocket (arugula) leaves, among others. Or we'd simply pick daisies and chamomile flowers and thread them into necklaces and crowns to wear on the way back home. Sometimes, the walk consisted of nothing but a change of scenery and a chance to secretly enjoy the sharp, tangy taste of soursob (*Oxalis pes-caprae*, or Bermuda buttercup), which I know many of my peers can relate to.

Lebanese people are resourceful when it comes to utilising foraged greens. I recently discovered that in some villages, not only do they stuff and roll vine

leaves, but also a certain type of mulberry leaves and those of the wild cyclamen as well. Times of unrest, war and shortage, even famine during the Ottoman occupation, made people look for ways to utilise and store foods for the longest periods of time without spoilage. In some villages, people store milk and yoghurt in heat-sealed glass bottles in their pantry to use in cooking. Meat is cooked and stored in salt and fat in jars. Vegetables and fruits are dried while others are preserved in oil, brine or sugar.

Classic Lebanese preserves had a resurgence a few years ago with the emergence of farmers' markets, like Beirut's Souk El Tayeb, where farmers and producers are encouraged to showcase and sell their products themselves. I've learned so much from chats with these producers who never shy away from sharing their knowledge with those curious to learn. As the market became saturated with similar jars of the usual jams and pickles, a few producers took it upon themselves to stand out and started experimenting with their products to elevate the quality or create new and inspiring flavours and techniques. An insurance broker uses her family's apple fields to produce naturally shelf-stable apple juice and uses it to sweeten her baked goods and jams. Another is known for the dehydrated fruits and jams she makes, others for vegan cheeses and spreads, nut butters, innovative sausages, or local brews and distilled drinks. This movement paved the way for several new producers to present locally made products that had previously been considered unusual, especially as they were so positively received.

The period of economic crisis that Lebanon has been going through has also sparked a trend towards replacing imported products with local ones. Locally made spirits and wines are on the rise, with superior quality and competitive prices, and many Lebanese wines have now won international awards.

AGED CHEESE DIP
Shanklish

For the balls

1 kg (4 cups) plain yoghurt

100 ml (scant ½ cup) water

½ teaspoon rock salt

To season

sea salt, to taste

red chilli powder, to taste

za'atar (*Za'atar Makhlout* – see page 206), to taste

For the dip

100 g (3½ oz) tomatoes, chopped

40 g (1½ oz) spring onions (scallions), finely sliced

handful of flat-leaf parsley, chopped

plenty of olive oil, for drizzling

To serve

soft or toasted pita bread

sliced vegetables of choice

Where do I begin to explain how much I love *shanklish*? *Shanklish* is an aged yoghurt, usually rolled into balls, and used rather like a soft cheese or made into a dip. I get the best *shanklish* from Akkar in North Lebanon, where it is fermented in clay pots until it's 'fully ripe'. This means that a crust of yeasts and mould has developed on the outside of the balls and the inside has acquired a beautiful sweet and sharp fermented taste that is similar to, but mellower than, blue cheese.

If you've never tasted the real thing before, the first time you try it you might find it rather pungent. If you're trying this recipe for the first time, skip the fermentation and go for the fresh spiced balls instead, which are known as *sourkeh* in Syria, before levelling up to fermented *shanklish*.

In the past year or so, with the extortionate increase in prices on imported goods into Lebanon, *shanklish* has made a good alternative to Parmesan in pasta dishes or pesto. Traditionally, we serve it as a layered dip dressed with a generous glug of olive oil and mixed at the table. The leftovers are delicious in wraps or warm ciabatta.

Combine the yoghurt, water and salt in a large saucepan and bring to the boil, stirring, then reduce the heat and simmer until the curds start to separate. Turn off the heat and let the mixture cool.

Pour the cooled mixture into a fine strainer or a cheesecloth (muslin) placed over a bowl or colander in the sink. Press most of the liquid out, then leave for a couple of hours to drain.

Take the strained curds (you should get around 185 g/6½ oz) and crumble them into a bowl. Season with salt, chilli powder and za'atar to taste (use extra salt if you plan to ferment the balls). Shape the curds into 4 balls of equal size, compressing each one tightly between your palms. Roll in more chilli or za'atar, as you like.

Leave the balls to air dry on a clean cotton dish towel, rotating occasionally, for 2–3 days. This is best done outside on hot, dry days, covered in a cloth to deter insects. A dry airing cupboard makes a good alternative.

To preserve the balls, either place them in a jar and cover with olive oil, or wrap tightly in clingfilm (plastic wrap). Refrigerate or freeze for later use.

Alternatively, you can ferment the *shanklish*. Once dried, place the balls in a clay pot to absorb moisture and keep in a dry, dark place for 1 month until they start to produce mould on their surfaces. Scrape off the mould with a knife and wash lightly in water, then roll in your spice of choice. They can then be wrapped in clingfilm and stored in the fridge or freezer until needed.

To make the dip, crumble 2 *shanklish* balls over a wide plate. Layer the tomatoes and spring onions on top, sprinkle with the parsley, then drown with olive oil. Serve with soft or toasted pita bread or sliced vegetables.

ROASTED CAULIFLOWER WITH BLACK & WHITE TAHINI

Arnabit Meshwe maa' Qizha w T-heene

Even though vegetarian food in Lebanese cuisine is plentiful, a fried cauliflower wrap has a special place in the hearts of vegetarians and carnivores alike. Almost every corner sandwich shop serves this delicious sandwich. I like this lighter, roasted version to serve as a side dish, as cauliflower tends to absorb oil and become soggy when fried. Blanching the cauli first helps it retain moisture.

Black tahini is not very common in Beirut, but is popular in south Lebanon and Palestine. It is made from *habbet el barake* (nigella seeds or black cumin), which means 'the blessings seed' for its nutritious qualities. For that, and for colour and a flavourful twist, I use both tahinis here, but feel free to use whatever you can find.

Preheat the oven to 200°C (400°F/gas 6). Line a baking sheet with baking paper.

Bring a pan of water to the boil, add the cauliflower and cook for 2 minutes, then drain and immediately plunge into iced water. Drain and dry.

In a large bowl, gently toss the florets with the olive oil, salt, cumin and garlic powder.

Arrange, well spaced, on the baking sheet and bake for 30 minutes, turning the florets halfway through cooking.

Meanwhile, prepare the white tahini sauce by mixing all the ingredients until well incorporated. Don't worry if the tahini breaks – keep whisking and it'll come together.

Repeat the process to make the black tahini sauce, if using.

Serve the roasted cauliflower florets on a large serving plate, drizzled with the two tahini sauces to make a stripy zebra pattern. Sprinkle with sesame seeds, pomegranate seeds and mint leaves and serve with lemon wedges on the side.

1 kg (2 lb 4 oz) cauliflower, broken into medium-sized florets

3 tablespoons olive oil

1 teaspoon sea salt

½ teaspoon ground cumin

½ teaspoon garlic powder

For the white tahini sauce
150 g (generous ½ cup) tahini

75 ml (5 tablespoons) cold water

100 ml (scant ½ cup) lemon juice

¼ teaspoon sea salt

For the black tahini sauce (optional)
100 g (⅓ cup) black tahini

50 g (3 tablespoons) tahini

75 ml (5 tablespoons) cold water

100 ml (scant ½ cup) lemon juice

¼ teaspoon sea salt

To serve
sesame seeds, for sprinkling

pomegranate seeds, for sprinkling

small handful of mint leaves

1 lemon, cut into wedges

CRISPY POTATOES WITH CORIANDER, GARLIC & CHILLI
Batata Harra

Even though this is a staple of Lebanese mezze, many a restaurant messes this up. It's either too soggy, or lacks flavour and chilli heat, or it's just fried potatoes with some seasonings. There was a place in Gemmayze, in a building that was sadly severely damaged by the explosion, where I loved the way they served it: crispy on the outside, soft on the inside, fragrant with coriander (cilantro), and with enough chilli to make it spicy but not unbearably hot.

For this recipe, I experimented a bit by trying different spice coatings – one dry, one wet – and the wet one was a clear winner. I also found that parboiling the potatoes ensures crispiness and texture on the outside while the insides are perfectly cooked and soft.

Bring the potatoes to the boil in a large pan of water and simmer until just cooked (until resistant to the point of a knife, but not completely soft). Drain and spread over plenty of paper towels to dry.

In a food processor, pulse the garlic and coriander, stems and all (reserving a few leaves for garnish), with the salt and olive oil until smooth. Transfer to a mixing bowl, stir in the pepper paste and chilli powder and set aside.

Heat an 8 cm (3 in) depth of oil in a deep-fryer or deep heavy-based saucepan to 180°C (350°F).

Fry the potatoes in small batches until golden, then remove with a slotted spoon to a clean mixing bowl. Add a couple of spoonfuls of the spice paste, to taste, and toss to coat. (Any leftover spice paste can be kept in a jar in the refrigerator, covered in a little olive oil, to use at a later date.)

Serve hot, garnished with the reserved coriander leaves and the chilli.

Pictured on page 91.

1 kg (2 lb 4 oz) potatoes, peeled and chopped into bite-sized cubes

20 g (¾ oz) garlic cloves, peeled

handful of fresh coriander (cilantro)

½ teaspoon salt

3 tablespoons olive oil

1 tablespoon red pepper paste

½ teaspoon chilli powder

vegetable oil, for frying

1 fresh red chilli, sliced (or a good pinch of dried chilli/red pepper flakes), to serve

TURNIP & BEETROOT PICKLES
Kabees Lefet w Shmandar

1 kg (2 lb 4 oz) turnips
300 g (10½ oz) beetroot (beets)
300 g (1 cup) rock salt
1 litre (4 cups) water

Pickling and fermenting are some of the traditional methods people used to preserve their excess seasonal produce. There is a difference between pickling, which usually is done in a vinegar solution, and fermenting, which is done in a simple salt brine. Salt brine encourages the growth of good bacteria, which ferments the preserved vegetables, while vinegar prohibits them. Vinegar-preserved vegetables usually last longer and are more stable, while salt-preserved ones reach a peak time for consumption and start to decline thereafter. I prefer salt brining for its gut-beneficial properties.

These pickles are a perfect match with falafel (see page 66) – their warm flavour complements the sandwich. If you're eating them as a side dish, their vibrant colour is always a great addition to any table. You will need to start making these at least 2 weeks before you want to eat them.

Clean and cut the turnips and beetroot into thick batons.

Prepare the pickling solution by mixing 250 g (¾ cup) of the salt into the water and stir until dissolved. Keep adding the rest of the salt until it is all combined. (Traditionally, people do the 'egg float test' here – test the salinity of the solution by gently dropping in a clean, fresh egg to see if it floats. If it doesn't, dissolve a little more salt in the solution until it does.)

Press the turnip and beetroot batons into sterilised jars (see page 224) and top with the pickling solution, making sure to completely cover the vegetables. Leave them open for a couple of hours, then seal and store for 2 weeks before consuming. Unopened, they will keep for up to a year. Once opened, store in the refrigerator and eat within about 12 weeks.

MARINATED STRING BEANS WITH GARLIC, WALNUTS & CHILLI
Makdous Loubye

1 kg (2 lb 4 oz) green (string) beans, ends and strings trimmed

3 garlic cloves

150 g (5 oz) shelled walnuts

3 tablespoons hot chilli paste

2 tablespoons rock salt

120 ml (½ cup) olive oil, plus extra for topping up (about 200 ml/ scant 1 cup per jar)

Skip making time-consuming stuffed eggplant (aubergine) *makdous* and go for *makdous loubye* – it's quicker and just as delicious. Traditionally, *mouneh*, or pantry preserves, are prepared to make the most of excess produce and this is no exception. Fresh garlic and string beans, and walnuts, chilli paste and olive oil from the previous year's harvest, are all pressed into a jar of goodness. I prepared this recipe to test out the proportions and gave a small sample to my family to try. I had to stop them, and myself, from going back to the bowl and finishing them off before I could press them into the jar! Here's a great trick though: use the same bowl, with the seasoning stuck to the sides, and some leftover beans that (intentionally) didn't fit into the jars, to mix a fresh salad and soak up every last bit of the spicy garlicky flavours.

Bring a large saucepan of water to the boil, drop the beans in and boil for 5 minutes. Drain and plunge into iced water to stop the cooking process.

Drain the beans in a strainer, then cover with a plate and a heavy weight (a kettle or a pot). Leave for at least 4 hours to remove excess moisture.

The next day, mash the garlic and crush the walnuts into small pieces. In a large bowl, mix the beans with the garlic, walnuts, chilli paste, salt and olive oil and toss to coat evenly.

Pack the mixture into jars and slowly top with more olive oil, making sure the oil seeps into the beans. Give each jar a little tap on the counter to help it settle and eliminate air pockets.

Leave the jars open for a few hours, add more oil if needed to keep the beans submerged, then seal.

The beans can be eaten immediately if they are soft, or used later as a side dish or snack, or on top of salads or a creamy plate of labneh. They keep well in a cool, dark place for around a year, as long as they are covered in oil, otherwise they'll get mouldy. Once the beans are consumed, use the oil in salad dressings or on top of labneh or hummus as your new secret spicy drizzle.

MAINS

Home-cooked stews are not easy to find in Beirut. Most restaurants in Lebanon, or abroad, take pride in serving proper *meza* and grilled meats, but lack the authenticity and comfort of those meals that remind us of home; of our moms stirring the big pot to feed the family, never following a recipe but trusting in her mother's teaching and her own heart and taste; of our grandma's years of experience, stretching her wrinkled hands to knead the traditional *kibbeh* mix with renewed strength; of our dads arranging the marinated meats onto skewers and taking charge of the grill and properly mixing the *arak* in the usual third-to-two-thirds ratio of spirit to water. Home-cooked food is about the comfort of shared food, of gatherings and stories and jokes and awkward moments with the family, even the uncles and aunts and cousins you don't really get along with.

The dishes in this chapter are those you will find in the home and are suited to being served for either lunch or dinner. Traditionally, the Lebanese are bigger on lunches, whereas dinners are usually lighter – some labneh and local white cheeses with lots of vegetables and olives and pickles. Maybe that's our secret to staying in good shape, despite consuming a lot of the good food available around us!

LAMB & BEAN STEW
Fasoulya w Riz

There are few practices from our ancestors that we still observe today, but our attitude to using meat in dishes has prevailed. Meat has always been considered a luxury. Farmers and cattle herders would only sacrifice an animal on special occasions: Easter, Eid al-Adha, a new birth, and so on. The meat had to be consumed quickly as there was no refrigeration, so it would be distributed to neighbours and family members. For the rest of the year, dishes would be prepared with little or no meat and this practice is still alive to this day – especially with the economic crisis Lebanon has been experiencing in recent years. When meat is used, it is celebrated and the flavour should be prominent. This stew is one of my favourites, with or without meat. It is typically made with a type of bean called *A'ayshe Khanom* (a variety of borlotti/cranberry bean), which arrive in midsummer and are ivory in colour with smudges of dark pink across them. If you can't find them, feel free to use regular borlotti or red kidney beans.

If using dried beans, soak them overnight in plenty of water. The next day, drain the beans and boil in fresh water for 15 minutes until just slightly cooked. Drain and set aside.

Add 1 tablespoon of the vegetable oil to a casserole (Dutch oven) over a medium-high heat, add the lamb shanks and sauté until lightly browned on all sides. Pour over enough water to cover, add the aromatics and season with salt. Cover and simmer for 30–40 minutes until the meat is cooked through, making sure to skim off and discard any scum from the top of the broth. Remove the meat and reserve the broth.

In the same pot, sauté the onions with the remaining vegetable oil until soft, then add the meat back to the pot along with the beans and 500 ml (2 cups) of the reserved broth to cover (topping it up with extra broth or water if needed). Bring to the boil, then reduce the heat and simmer, covered, until the beans are cooked, around 30 minutes.

Dilute the tomato paste in a little water and stir into the pot. In a small pan, sauté the pesto with the olive oil and cumin for 2–3 minutes until fragrant (don't let it catch and burn), then stir into the pot.

Remove from the heat and let rest for 5 minutes. Serve with rice pilaf or pita bread.

350 g (2 generous cups) dried borlotti/cranberry or red kidney beans (or 600 g/scant 4 cups cooked beans)

2 tablespoons vegetable oil

200 g (7 oz) lamb shanks, cubed

½ teaspoon ground nutmeg

1 teaspoon allspice or 1 cinnamon stick

2 bay leaves

200 g (7 oz) onions, sliced

3 tablespoons tomato paste

2 heaped tablespoons Coriander and Garlic Pesto (page 209)

1 tablespoon olive oil

1 tablespoon ground cumin

salt, to taste

pita bread or Basic Pilaf (page 208), to serve (optional)

KOFTA, POTATO & TOMATO CASSEROLE
Kafta w Batata Bil Sayniye

800 g (1 lb 12 oz) potatoes, peeled and sliced into discs 1 cm (½ in) thick

300 g (10½ oz) onions, sliced into discs 1 cm (½ in) thick

300 g (10½ oz) tomatoes, sliced into discs 1 cm (½ in) thick

2 tablespoons tomato paste

1 teaspoon salt

300 ml (1¼ cups) freshly boiled water

pita bread or Basic Pilaf (page 208), to serve (optional)

For the kofta

1 kg (2 lb 4 oz) minced (ground) beef (10% fat)

200 g (7 oz) onion, grated or finely chopped

handful of flat-leaf parsley, finely chopped

1½ teaspoons salt

1 tablespoon allspice

Long before ovens were in every home, there was the neighbourhood bakery, where women in the city (back then, they were the ones in charge of cooking) would take their trays of food to be baked for lunch. The bakery was a social hub – a place for women to gather, make flatbreads and share a few stories (perhaps about the neighbour they had some good gossip about, or to boast about their childrens', husbands' or relatives' achievements) while they waited for their lunch to be baked. It gave rise to the phrase *neswen el forn* (the ladies of the bakery), typically used to describe someone who could not keep a secret. Men would gather in coffee shops or barber shops and complain about how women gossiped and couldn't keep secrets, while they themselves talked about everyone else. At least the time at the bakery ended with a delicious casserole on top of a couple of new stories to share!

This casserole is rich and comforting, and easy to prepare. Just cut and layer your ingredients and let the oven do all the work for you, while you have a video call with your family or friends to get all the latest gossip.

Preheat the oven to 180°C (350°F/gas 4).

Start by making the kofta. In a large bowl, mix the beef with the onion, parsley, salt and allspice until well combined. Do not overwork the mixture as it will become tough. Lightly press the kofta mixture into the bottom of a large casserole dish (Dutch oven) to form an even layer, about 2 cm (¾ in) deep. Bake for 15 minutes until almost cooked and slightly shrunken.

Meanwhile, parboil the potatoes until slightly fork tender and drain.

Layer the potatoes on top of the kofta mixture in the casserole, followed by a layer of the onions and tomatoes, or mix up the layering of the vegetables as you wish.

Dilute the tomato paste and salt in the boiled water and pour into the casserole dish – it should barely cover the ingredients. Return to the oven to bake for a further 20–30 minutes until the vegetables are cooked and starting to char around the edges.

Serve immediately with pita bread or rice pilaf.

MEATBALLS & ONIONS IN TOMATO SAUCE
Daoud Bacha

For the meatballs

800 g (1 lb 12 oz) coarsely minced (ground) beef (10% fat)

100 g (3½ oz) onions, finely sliced

handful of flat-leaf parsley, finely chopped

½ teaspoon allspice

1 teaspoon salt

3 tablespoons vegetable oil

For the sauce

2 tablespoons vegetable oil

500 g (1 lb 2 oz) onions, thinly sliced

4 garlic cloves, thinly sliced

750 g (1 lb 10 oz) fresh tomatoes, grated (take care to keep all of the juices)

1 tablespoon tomato paste (optional)

1 teaspoon salt

To serve

Basic Pilaf (page 208)

The origin of this popular Levantine dish is commonly attributed to an Ottoman ruler or *Pasha* who loved eating this dish every day. The dish evolved regionally with different variations: some add potatoes to stretch out and reduce the meat quantity and make it more filling, while others flavour the tomato sauce with pomegranate molasses. Pine nuts are also an optional addition to level up this recipe.

This is the classic version, but I do suggest you try adding some starchy potato cubes that have first been fried until lightly golden and then finished in the sauce.

First, make the meatballs. In a large bowl, mix the beef with the onions, parsley, allspice and salt until combined, then form into meatballs, about 4 cm (1½ in) in diameter.

In a shallow frying pan (skillet), heat the vegetable oil over a medium heat and fry the meatballs for 6–8 minutes until browned and cooked on all sides, then remove and set aside.

In a large casserole (Dutch oven), heat the vegetable oil over a medium-high heat, add the onions and garlic and sauté until slightly translucent. Add the meatballs and mix well. Add the grated tomatoes and their juices to the pot, season with the salt, then add 2 cups of water, or enough to cover the meatballs. If the tomatoes aren't ripe enough and lack flavour, dilute the tomato paste in a little water and stir into the pot. Bring to the boil, then reduce the heat and simmer, partially covered with a lid, for 30 minutes until the sauce has thickened.

Serve with a rice pilaf.

KIBBEH IN TAHINI STEW
Kibbeh Arnabiye

There are many different versions of this dish: some use whole onions, others add chickpeas, and some make hollow *kibbeh* balls to serve with lamb shanks with the sauce. However, the one distinguishing ingredient is the bitter orange juice that gives the sauce its unique flavour.

This stew is considered a feast dish and is made in large quantities for gatherings. Beirutis make it to celebrate the change of the seasons. In mid-winter, bitter oranges and other citrus fruits harvested from all over the Lebanese coast fill the produce shops. We make the most of them and freeze the bitter orange juice for later use (it is also an ingredient in *Ful Mdammas*, page 21). If you can't find bitter oranges, try using Valencia oranges, clementines or tangerines. My friend Iffat recalls her family making this with the juice of seven different citrus fruits, which lightens the rather heavy tahini sauce. If you're feeling a bit adventurous, add a teaspoon of orange blossom water, which is made from the blossoms of bitter oranges, to the sauce for a whole new aromatic experience.

First, make the *kibbeh* mixture. Place the bulgur in a bowl with enough water to cover and set aside to soak while you prepare the meat.

In a large bowl, mix together the beef, onion, salt and spices until well combined. Drain the bulgur if any water remains unabsorbed and mix with the beef until well combined. Alternatively – especially if you can't get finely minced beef – combine the ingredients in a food processor. Cover and chill in the refrigerator.

Next, make the filling. Heat the olive oil in a saucepan over a medium heat and fry the pine nuts until golden. Scoop out and set aside. In the same pan, sauté the onion for 5–7 minutes until translucent. Add the salt and spices, then add the beef and sauté until browned. Add half of the reserved pine nuts back to the pan and stir though, then leave to cool.

Preheat the oven to 180°C (350°F/gas 4).

To make the kibbeh balls, wet your hand in a bowl of cold water and take a small ball of the kibbeh mixture, slightly larger than a ping-pong ball.

For the *kibbeh*
250 g (scant 1½ cups) fine bulgur wheat

400 g (14 oz) finely minced (ground) beef

50 g (2 oz) onion, grated

1 teaspoon salt

1 teaspoon ground cinnamon

1 teaspoon allspice

¼ teaspoon ground nutmeg

For the filling
2 tablespoons olive oil, plus extra for brushing

40 g (⅓ cup) pine nuts

200 g (7 oz) onion, chopped

1 teaspoon salt

½ teaspoon ground cinnamon

½ teaspoon allspice

¼ teaspoon ground nutmeg

200 g (7 oz) finely minced (ground) beef

For the sauce
2 tablespoons olive oil

250 g (9 oz) onion, grated

2 garlic cloves, grated

750 ml (3 cups) water

270 g (1 cup) tahini

500–650 ml (2–2½ cups) citrus juice (I use 300 ml/1¼ cups bitter orange juice and make up the remainder with a mix of Valencia oranges and clementines)

1 teaspoon salt, or to taste

1 teaspoon orange blossom water, or to taste (optional)

To serve
Basic Pilaf (page 208)

Roll it in your palms, then poke a hole in it with one finger. Use your finger to press against the sides, turning as you go, until you have a hollow, thin-sided shell. Spoon in 1 teaspoonful of the filling mixture and seal the edges. Compress each ball well and mould into a rugby-ball shape – with a point at each end. Alternatively, flatten the ball against your wet palm, spoon in the filling, carefully bring in the sides to enclose it into a ball, then press into the classic pointed shape. Repeat until you have used up all the mixture – it should make about 30 *kibbeh* balls.

Place on a baking sheet, brush the *kibbeh* with olive oil and bake in the oven for 15 minutes, flipping once. Some people prefer to cook them in the sauce, but I prefer that they firm up before adding them to the sauce.

To make the sauce, heat the olive oil in a small saucepan over a medium heat and sauté the onion for 10–12 minutes until amber in colour (or the colour of a wasp's wings as directed by Iffat's mother). Add the garlic and cook for 1 minute, then pour in 500 ml (2 cups) of the water and simmer for 20–30 minutes until soft.

In a bowl, dilute the tahini with the remaining 250 ml (1 cup) of water and add 500ml (2 cups) of the citrus juices and 1 teaspoon of salt.

When the onions are cooked through, stir in the tahini sauce, bring to the boil, then reduce the heat and simmer for 20–30 minutes, stirring often, until the mixture starts to thicken. Taste and adjust the seasoning, adding more juice to loosen it up or spike up the flavour. Add the orange blossom water to taste, if using.

Add the *kibbeh* balls to the sauce and allow them to heat through before serving with rice pilaf, sprinkled with the remaining golden pine nuts.

SHEET-PAN 'STUFFED' KIBBEH
Kibbeh Bil Sayniye

For the raw *kibbeh* mixture

600 g (1 lb 5 oz) finely minced (ground)
    lean beef

50 g (2 oz) onion, finely grated

450 g (2¾ cups) fine whole-wheat
    bulgur wheat, rinsed and drained

6 basil leaves, finely chopped

2 sprigs of mint, finely chopped

2 sprigs of marjoram, finely chopped

¾ teaspoon allspice

½ teaspoon ground nutmeg

1½ teaspoons salt

200 ml (generous ¾ cup) cold water

For the 'cooked' filling mixture

80 ml (⅓ cup) olive oil

20 g (3 tablespoons) pine nuts

200 g (7 oz) onion, finely chopped

200 g (7 oz) minced (ground) beef

½ teaspoon salt

¼ teaspoon ground nutmeg

½ teaspoon allspice

3 tablespoons vegetable oil or
    melted ghee

To serve

Cucumber and Yoghurt Salad (page 81)
    or Zesty Cabbage Salad (page 82)

A classic! An excellent way to stretch meat and create an interesting dish. Some families serve this as a main for holiday lunches or Sunday gatherings. It is similar to *kibbeh nayye* (raw *kibbeh*), although it is slightly less spiced and with a higher fat content for better flavour. Some people mix leftover *kibbeh nayye* with extra bulgur and spices to bake the next day as a traybake. This makes sense to me, since I grew up pairing raw *kibbeh* with what we call *haousé*, which is basically the 'cooked' filling part of this recipe. It was years before I discovered that this was only done by the Palestinian side of my family.

You can get creative and make your own patterns on top of the *kibbeh* – the cut lines make excellent portion dividers and crisp up nicely once oiled and baked. A refreshing salad makes the best accompaniment.

Preheat the oven to 180°C (350°F/gas 4).

In a large bowl, combine all the raw *kibbeh* ingredients and knead by hand until well combined. Set aside for 20–30 minutes to soften and marinate.

For the filling, heat the olive oil in a frying pan (skillet) over a medium heat and fry the pine nuts until golden. Scoop out and set aside. Add the onion to the pan and fry until translucent, then add the beef, salt and spices and cook until the meat is browned. Mix the pine nuts back in and leave to cool.

Brush the bottom and sides of a 24 cm (9½ in) round deep baking tray/ sheet pan or a casserole dish (Dutch oven) with vegetable oil. With damp hands, press half of the raw *kibbeh* mix into the dish in an even layer. Top with the filling mixture, then cover with the remaining raw *kibbeh*. To help spread it over the soft filling mixture, dampen your hands, shape a portion of raw *kibbeh* like a patty and lay it on top of the filling. Repeat until the *kibbeh* is finished and the filling is completely covered. Press with the heels of your palms until it forms an even layer. Use a sharp knife to cut the mixture into about 8 sections and score each section with a pattern of your choice – I usually score concentric circles, then cross it with a geometric pattern. Poke a hole in the middle of the mixture with your finger or the end of a wooden spoon. Pour the vegetable oil or melted ghee into the hole, allowing it to overflow, and tilt the dish/tray until all of the *kibbeh* is covered with oil.

Bake in the hot oven for 30 minutes.

Meanwhile, heat the grill (broiler) to high, then transfer the baked *kibbeh* to the grill for a final 5 minutes to brown the top.

When cooked, 'shock' the *kibbeh* by sprinkling it with a little cold water. This keeps the top nice and soft. Serve immediately, with a refreshing salad.

STUFFED CABBAGE ROLLS
Malfouf Mehshe

My family aren't in agreement on whether this is a main meal or an appetiser – some claim it is not filling enough on its own and needs other dishes on the side. Regardless, it is delicious and you'll want more than one serving. Most people overcook the cabbage until it's barely holding up and the rice absorbs so much water that it's falling apart, but I like a bit of texture and a very slight bite to the cabbage and rice. Layer some unpeeled garlic cloves in between the rolls and you can squeeze them out of their skins and enjoy with an extra squeeze of lemon.

Start by soaking the rice for the filling in water for 15–20 minutes.

Carve the stem out of the bottom of the cabbage and try to separate the leaves, at least the outer ones, as much as you can without cutting them Bring a large pan of water to the boil and blanch the leaves for 3 minutes, or until softened and changed in colour. Drain and press them in the strainer to remove excess water. Leave to cool a little.

To make the filling, drain the soaked rice and place in a large bowl. Add the beef, cinnamon, allspice, nutmeg and fine salt, and mix to combine.

Take the largest cabbage leaves and cut out the thick stems. Lay the stems in the bottom of a large casserole dish (Dutch oven). Place 4–5 cloves of garlic on top of the stems.

To begin stuffing, lay the leaves out, veiny side up, with the longest side facing you. Spread a heaped tablespoon of the filling in a line in the quarter of the leaf that's closest to you and fold the long side over to enclose the filling. Roll into a long, thin cigar shape with just enough pressure to not to let the filling squeeze out of the sides. Arrange the stuffed rolls in the pot, and dot each layer with more garlic cloves. For the smaller leaves, you can combine 2 small pieces to make a larger piece that you can roll together.

Stir the sea salt and cumin into the measured water and pour all over the cabbage rolls, then cover with a heatproof plate to weigh the rolls down. Place the pot on the heat, cover with the lid and bring to the boil, then reduce the heat and simmer for 30 minutes until the rice is cooked through.

To finish, mix the lemon juice and mint and drizzle over the cabbage rolls. Serve as they are, or with some tangy yoghurt on the side or drizzled over.

1 large white (green) cabbage (about 1.4 kg/3 lb)

3 whole heads of garlic, separated into cloves (skins left on)

1 teaspoon sea salt

1 tablespoon ground cumin

600 ml (2½ cups) water

60 ml (¼ cup) freshly squeezed lemon juice

1 tablespoon dried mint

plain yoghurt, to serve (optional)

For the filling

370 g (2 cups) Egyptian short-grain rice

500 g (1 lb 2 oz) finely minced (ground) lean beef

1 teaspoon ground cinnamon

1 teaspoon allspice

¼ teaspoon ground nutmeg

1 teaspoon fine salt

MOLOKHIA & CHICKEN STEW WITH RICE
Mloukhiye w Riz

Molokhia (*mloukhiye* in Lebanese) are the leaves from a plant called Jew's mallow (*Corchorus olitorius*), a crop that fills grocers with its long leafy stalks in late summer. In my family, we always prefer fresh or frozen over dried leaves, but feel free to use dried if that's all you can find (you'll need less than the frozen amount).

This is a warming dish for both stomach and heart, as it is filling and nutritious, rich in vitamins and iron. But it's also a dish with so many variations. A friend living in Palestine told me that they can tell whether a Palestinian is Christian or Muslim by the way they prepare *mloukhiye*. Muslims cook it with the leaves finely chopped into a sort of slimy stew, while Christians cook the leaves whole. Give us a plant and we'll find a way to divide ourselves over it!

Put the chicken, vegetables, lemon zest, whole spices and salt into a large stockpot and pour over enough water to cover. Bring to the boil and skim off and discard the foam, then cover, reduce the heat and simmer for 1 hour.

After 1 hour, remove the chicken, let it cool slightly, then remove all the meat from the bones and set aside. Strain the cooking broth and set aside.

Pound the garlic in a pestle and mortar with a little salt until smooth.

In a large casserole (Dutch oven), heat the olive oil over a medium heat. Add the coriander and garlic and cook until fragrant. Remove half of the mixture and set aside. Add the molokhia, pour in 2–3 litres (8–12 cups) of the reserved chicken broth (enough to cover) and taste for seasoning. Bring to the boil, then reduce the heat and simmer for 15 minutes. Don't stir much – stirring will make the molokhia too glutinous. Just before turning off the heat, stir in the reserved coriander and garlic and the chicken meat.

Meanwhile, make the rice. Heat the olive oil in a small saucepan, add the rice and sauté for a minute, then add 750 ml (3 cups) of the chicken broth. Cover, bring to the boil, then reduce the heat and simmer for 20 minutes. Turn off the heat, fluff the rice, then cover and let it rest for 5 minutes.

Serve the stew with the rice, toasted pita bread and lemon juice or apple cider vinegar mixed with diced red onion.

For the poached chicken and broth
1 whole chicken (1.2 kg/2 lb 12 oz)

1 medium onion, halved

1 carrot, halved

pared zest of 1 lemon

½ piece of whole nutmeg

2 cinnamon sticks

3 bay leaves

2 whole cloves

2 cardamom pods

1 tablespoon fine salt

For the molokhia stew
1 head of garlic (40 g/1½ oz), cloves separated and peeled

pinch of sea salt

2 tablespoons olive oil

large bunch of coriander (cilantro) (about 150 g/5 oz), finely chopped

700 g (1 lb 9 oz) frozen molokhia

For the rice
400 g (2 cups) long-grain rice

1 teaspoon fine salt

2 tablespoons olive oil

To serve
toasted pita bread

lemon wedges, for squeezing

120 ml (½ cup) lemon juice or apple cider vinegar (optional)

1 medium red onion, diced (optional)

CHICKEN FATTÉ
Fattet Djej

200 g (scant 1 cup) dried chickpeas (garbanzo beans) or 1 x 400 g (14 oz) tinned

2 chicken breasts

4 tablespoons olive oil

4 tablespoons butter

2 garlic cloves

½ teaspoon salt

500 g (2 cups) plain yoghurt

1 teaspoon garlic powder

4 tablespoons tahini

2 pita breads

50 g (⅔ cup) slivered almonds

50 g (scant ½ cup) cashews

2 teaspoons ground cumin

2 teaspoons paprika

small handful of flat-leaf parsley, chopped

For the marinade

60 ml (¼ cup) olive oil

1 teaspoon salt

½ teaspoon white pepper

1 teaspoon paprika

zest of 1 lemon

This recipe has several different origins and variations and is excellent for using up leftovers. While the *fatteh* in the breakfast section (page 18) is enjoyed mostly in the mornings or for brunch, this version is more of a lunch or dinner item. The tahini yoghurt sauce gives it a deeper and richer taste, and the garlic powder brings a sweeter taste to complement the pungent flavour of the fresh garlic. A Palestinian version of *fatté* also includes rice and vermicelli pilaf. You can use leftover rotisserie chicken, reheated and flavoured with the spices in this recipe, or marinate and grill a fresh batch.

If using dried chickpeas, soak them overnight in plenty of water.

The next day, drain the chickpeas, place in a saucepan and cover with plenty of fresh water. Bring to the boil, then skim off the foam with a slotted spoon. Reduce the heat and simmer for 60–80 minutes until the chickpeas are cooked and tender. Drain and rinse in cold water and set aside to cool slightly. If using tinned chickpeas, simply drain and heat through.

Butterfly each chicken breast with a horizontal cut through the middle. Mix together the marinade ingredients and rub the mixture all over the chicken. Marinate for at least 20 minutes, but ideally 2 hours or even overnight.

Heat half of the olive oil with half of the butter in a sauté pan over a high heat and fry the chicken breasts on both sides until cooked through and with a nice crust on the outside (alternatively, grill them). Leave to rest for 5 minutes before cutting into strips or bite-sized cubes.

Mash the garlic with the salt in a pestle and mortar. Transfer to a bowl and mix with the yoghurt, garlic powder and tahini until incorporated.

Toast or fry the pita breads and break them into large chunks.

Heat the remaining oil and butter in a pan and fry the nuts until golden.

Place the pita pieces at the bottom of a glass serving dish. Layer the cooked chickpeas on top and cover with the tahini yoghurt. Place the chicken pieces on top. Pour the nuts, including their hot buttery oils, all over the *fatté* and sprinkle with the cumin, paprika and parsley. Serve immediately.

CHICKEN & POTATO TRAYBAKE WITH LEMON & GARLIC DRESSING

Djej w Batata Maa' Toom w Hamod

On days when you just need a good quick fix, this dish comes to the rescue. Simple comfort food with accessible ingredients and the least cooking possible. There is something comforting for me in the flavours of garlic and lemon – they taste like home; a happy memory of home. We'd have this dish for lunch with nothing but a basic salad on the side and lots of thin soft bread to wrap bite-sized pieces of chicken and potatoes moistened with the lemon and garlic sauce. For me, this dish is a whole sensory experience, from the fragrant smell to the delicious appearance, followed by touch and taste. My mom would sometimes stray away from the traditional flavours and sprinkle over some dried thyme to give the dish a different dimension.

Preheat the oven to 180°C (350°F/gas 4).

Rub the chicken pieces with the halved lemon, white pepper, nutmeg, 2 teaspoons of salt and half of the olive oil. Place the chicken pieces in a roasting pan and bake for 15–20 minutes.

Meanwhile, boil the potato wedges in a large pan of salted water for about 15 minutes, or until fork tender. Drain and add to the chicken tray.

Pound the garlic together with about 1 teaspoon of salt in a pestle and mortar until creamy, then transfer to a bowl and mix with the coriander, lemon juice and the remaining olive oil.

Drizzle the dressing over the chicken and potatoes, ensuring everything is well coated, and return to the oven for a further 30 minutes, or until the potatoes start to brown and crisp around the edges.

Serve with pita bread for scooping.

2 kg (4 lb 8 oz) chicken (whole, breast, thighs or a mix), cut into pieces if using whole

1 lemon, halved

1 teaspoon white pepper

½ teaspoon ground nutmeg

250 ml (1 cup) olive oil

2 kg (4 lb 8 oz) potatoes, peeled and cut into wedges

100 g (3½ oz) garlic

bunch of (about 50 g/2 oz) coriander (cilantro), finely chopped

250 ml (1 cup) lemon juice

salt

pita bread, to serve

CHICKEN, SUMAC & CARAMELISED ONION ROLLS
Msakhan

I find one of the best introductions to a country's culture is through its food. Dig deeper and get into the origins of recipes and you'll find routes of people immigrating and influencing and in turn being influenced by the region they live in. *Msakhan* is not a Beiruti dish, nor it is Lebanese, but it became a common *meza* dish because of Palestinian influence. Palestinians have lived in Lebanon since they were expelled from their homeland in 1948. Many families kept cooking and passing down their recipes and some evolved with time, like this one.

Originally prepared to use up leftover *taboon* bread (a traditional bread similar to *tannour/tandoor*), the bread would be rubbed with good olive oil, then used to wrap a whole spiced raw chicken and plenty of sumac-rubbed onions, then roasted. The bread soaks up the spices, juices and fat from the chicken and becomes soft and pliable enough to grab pieces of chicken and onions, and wrap them to put in your mouth. These days, it is made with pre-cooked shredded chicken meat and *saj/markouk* bread, a thin crêpe-like bread, and baked until crispy.

My mom would make this recipe and use the broth from the poached chicken to make a simple chicken soup to go with it.

First, poach the chicken. Put the chicken, vegetables, lemon zest, whole spices and salt into a large stockpot and pour over enough water to cover. Bring to the boil and skim off and discard the foam that rises to the top. Cover, reduce the heat and simmer for 1 hour.

After 1 hour, remove the chicken, let it cool slightly, then remove all the meat from the bones, shred and set aside in a bowl. (Strain the cooking broth and keep for another recipe.)

Heat the oil in a large saucepan over a medium heat, add the onions and gently fry for about 20 minutes until softened and caramelised but still pale golden in colour. Remove with a slotted spoon to the bowl with the chicken, reserving the oil.

Meanwhile, preheat the oven to 180°C (350°F/gas 4). Line a baking sheet with baking paper.

For the poached chicken

1 whole chicken (1.2 kg/2 lb 12 oz)

1 medium onion, halved

1 carrot, halved

pared zest of 1 lemon

½ piece nutmeg

2 cinnamon sticks

3 bay leaves

2 whole cloves

2 cardamom pods

1 tablespoon salt

To finish

120 ml (½ cup) olive oil

1 kg (2 lb 4 oz) onions, thinly sliced

2 tablespoons sumac

4–5 thin saj breads

To serve

pomegranate molasses, for drizzling

Cucumber and Yoghurt Salad (page 81), to serve

Mix the caramelised onions and shredded chicken with the sumac.

Cut the bread into large triangles (around 15 x 20 cm/6 x 8 in). Place a triangle on the work surface with the longest edge facing you. Fill the middle with a tablespoon of the chicken and onion filling and fold the long side of the triangle over to cover, fold in the sides to seal the ends, and continue to roll tightly towards the point of the triangle. Use a toothpick to hold it in place or just place on the lined baking sheet with the flap facing down. Continue to fill the wraps until the filling runs out. Brush the rolls with the reserved cooking oil (it can be used for starting any recipe as well – it has a beautiful onion flavour).

Bake for 10 minutes until the rolls are crispy and well browned.

Serve immediately, drizzled with pomegranate molasses, with a cucumber and yoghurt salad on the side.

BEIRUTI FISH PILAF
Sayyadiye

1 x 650 g (1 lb 7 oz) gilt-head bream (or 2 smaller ones), scaled and gutted (ask your fishmonger)

vegetable oil, for frying

600 g (1 lb 5 oz) onions, thinly sliced

1 carrot, halved

2 bay leaves

1 cinnamon stick

2 large pared strips of lemon zest

1 cardamom pod

2 whole cloves

¼ whole nutmeg

400 g (2 cups) basmati or other long-grain rice, rinsed and drained

1 tablespoon ground coriander

1 teaspoon ground cinnamon

1 teaspoon allspice

1 teaspoon caraway seeds

50 g (⅓ cup) plain (all-purpose) flour

sea salt, to taste

For the gravy (optional)

2–3 tablespoons plain (all-purpose) flour (or cornflour/cornstarch)

2 tablespoons double (heavy) cream (optional)

salt and pepper, to taste

The wonderful flavours of this dish come from the fish broth and the caramelised onions that are cooked in it, as well as from the spices in the rice. Textures come into play, too: the fluffy rice is topped with soft pieces of fish, then garnished with more of those crispy onions (some people add fried nuts, too). It's all bound together with a delicious, creamy gravy. This is definitely one of my favourites.

If the fish is large, score the skin and season with 1½ teaspoons sea salt. Heat a good splash of vegetable oil in a deep sauté pan over a medium-high heat, add the fish and fry on both sides until cooked through, about 5–6 minutes (depending on the size of the fish). Drain and cool on paper towels, then pick the meat from the fish and set aside. Reserve the carcass.

Add 3 tablespoons of vegetable oil to a large stockpot, add 350 g (12 oz) of the onions and sauté until deeply caramelised but not charred. Remove half of the onions and set aside to drain on paper towels.

Drain the excess oil from the pot, then add the fish carcass, carrot, bay leaves, cinnamon, lemon zest, cardamom, cloves, nutmeg and enough water to completely cover (at least 1.5 litres/6 cups). Bring to the boil, then reduce the heat and simmer for 45 minutes–1 hour. Strain and reserve the stock.

Heat 1 tablespoon of vegetable oil in a large casserole (Dutch oven) over a medium-high heat, add the rice and sauté for 1–2 minutes. Add the caramelised onions, 600 ml (2½ cups) of the fish stock, the ground spices, caraway seeds and ¾ teaspoon of salt, and stir to combine. Bring to the boil, then reduce the heat to low, cover, and simmer for 10 minutes. Arrange the flaked fish on top of the rice, add a bit more stock (if the rice looks too dry), then re-cover and cook for another 10 minutes. Remove from the heat and leave to rest for 5 minutes.

Meanwhile, heat an 8 cm (3 in) depth of oil in a deep-fryer or deep heavy-based saucepan to 180°C (350°F). Toss the remaining uncooked onions in the flour and shake off the excess. Deep-fry the onions in small batches until golden and crispy. Remove to drain on paper towels and set aside.

If desired, use any remaining stock to make a gravy to serve on the side. You should have about 500 ml (2 cups) of stock left. Whisk 2 tablespoons of flour into the cold stock in a saucepan, then place over a medium heat and whisk constantly until thickened. Add a bit more flour, if needed. Taste and adjust the seasoning. You could also stir in a little cream after it thickens, but it's not traditional.

To serve, fluff the rice and spread the pilaf over a large serving plate. Top with the crispy onions and serve, with the gravy on the side, if wished.

ROASTED FISH WITH A SPICY SAUCE
Samke Harra

2 lemons, thinly sliced

2 onions (about 500 g/1 lb 2 oz), sliced

4 large tomatoes (about 400 g/14 oz), halved or cut into quarters

4 bell peppers (about 300 g/10½ oz), deseeded and cut into large chunks

40 g (1½ oz) chillies, halved and deseeded

80 g (3 oz) garlic cloves

50 g (2 oz) fresh coriander (cilantro)

2 teaspoons sea salt, plus extra to taste

60 ml (¼ cup) olive oil, or more as needed

1 x 1.7–2 kg (3 lb 12 oz–4 lb 8 oz) sea bass or cod (or 2 smaller ones), gutted, cleaned and dried

pita or flatbreads, to serve (optional)

I always wondered why we didn't do more with some of the ingredients we have here. For example, the most common way of preparing fish at home is just grilled with a twist of lemon, or flour-coated and fried with *tarator* (tahini sauce). It was only later that I realised that this was because of the freshness of the fish we get – the other ingredients only need to complement it rather than overpower it.

This recipe is common in Ras Beirut, where many men's pastime is to take their fishing rods and a small foldable chair and spend the morning or afternoon by the water, a few steps down from the Manara (lighthouse) seaside corniche, a popular spot for joggers, cyclists, couples on dates, old men chatting about politics, or families walking with their children.

Samke harra is a feast dish suitable for gatherings (look for a meaty fish), and the garnished fish is a head-turner and a palate awakener. The bright aromas of lemon, coriander (cilantro) and garlic bring out the flavour of the fish, and the warm spicy sauce adds an extra kick!

Preheat the oven to 200°C (400°F/gas 6).

Line a roasting pan with baking paper or kitchen foil and arrange the sliced lemons, onions, tomatoes, peppers and chillies over the surface.

In a food processor, pulse the peeled garlic and coriander with 2 teaspoons of salt and the olive oil until it creates a paste. Stuff the cavity of the fish with three-quarters of the paste. Brush the remaining paste over the skin of the fish, along with an extra drizzle of olive oil, if needed. Lay the fish on top of the vegetables and cover with foil.

Bake for 20 minutes, then remove the foil and bake for a further 10–15 minutes.

Remove from the oven and carefully set the fish to one side. Let cool slightly until you can handle the vegetables, then remove and discard the lemon slices and peel the skins from the tomatoes, peppers and chillies. Chop the skinned roasted vegetables finely on a chopping board, then mix them together. Season to taste with salt.

Serve the vegetable sauce on top of the fish or on the side, with the bread.

GRILLED OCTOPUS WITH CORIANDER & GARLIC & A MOGHRABIEH SALAD
Akhtabout Meshwe w Salatet Moghrabieh

1 kg (2 lb 4 oz) octopus (1 large or 2–3 small), cleaned

4 bay leaves

pared zest of 1 lemon

250 ml (1 cup) white wine

60 ml (¼ cup) olive oil

2 tablespoons paprika

3 tablespoons Coriander and Garlic Pesto (page 209)

2 tablespoons lemon juice

½ teaspoon salt

2 tablespoons sherry (or white wine)

For the moghrabieh salad

330 g (2 cups) cooked moghrabieh/ maftoul pearl couscous (giant couscous)

2 ripe tomatoes, deseeded and diced

2 tablespoons Coriander and Garlic Pesto (page 209)

½ teaspoon salt

60 ml (¼ cup) lemon juice

Despite being a port city in a Mediterranean country, seafood is not the first thing you might think of when considering Beiruti or Lebanese cuisine. Mostly this is because, as I have mentioned before, we tend to let the star ingredient shine by itself rather than dress it up. However, a few restaurants have started to work with seafood and develop new recipes. This recipe is a combination of two dishes I've tried in Baron, a hip and popular restaurant in Mar Mikhael that uses local ingredients in new ways, with modern cooking techniques and creative presentation. The octopus is twice cooked – the first time to cook it through and tenderise it; the second to get the char and nice crispy bits around the edges. Inspired by the restaurant's presentation, I've used the moghrabieh pearls in a way that people don't do at home: cold in a salad, rather than in a stew. I'm sure this will offend some traditionalists!

Put the octopus into a stockpot, add the bay leaves, lemon zest, white wine and enough water to cover. Gently bring to a simmer, then cook over a low heat for about 1 hour 20 minutes, depending on the size of the octopus. If using a large octopus, it might take more time; if using 2–3 small ones, it'll take less. Test by inserting a knife into the fleshy part of the tentacles; if it slides in easily, it is done. Take the pot off the heat and allow the octopus to cool in the water.

Once cooled, separate the tentacles with a knife or kitchen scissors. Place in a bowl and mix with the olive oil, paprika, pesto, lemon juice and salt. Let it marinate for at least 1 hour or overnight in the refrigerator, if possible.

To make the salad, mix the cooked moghrabieh pearls with the tomatoes and the pesto, and season with the salt and lemon juice, to taste. Spread over a serving dish.

When ready to serve, heat a grill pan over a high heat and grill the marinated octopus on both sides until slightly charred. Carefully, pour over the sherry or wine (the alcohol might catch and flame) and let it bubble a bit to deglaze the pan.

Serve the grilled octopus on top of the moghrabieh salad.

SPINACH DUMPLINGS IN A GARLIC & MINT YOGHURT SAUCE
Shish Barak Sbanekh bil Laban

SERVES 4–5

As a kid, I remember watching my mom and grandma gather around large oiled trays, with rolling pins, one or two water glasses, and large bowls of dough and prepared raw filling. They'd allow us to help with simple tasks, such as cutting the rolled dough with the rim of the glass or arranging the filled dumplings in the trays. They'd be preparing a large pot of *shish barak* (lamb dumplings in a yoghurt sauce) as a warming lunch for the family, and we'd steal the golden and crunchy dumplings as soon as they were out of the oven.

Similar dishes can be found all across central Asia and the Middle East, but meat-filled dumplings in a hot garlicky, minty yoghurt is most common in the Levant. For this recipe, I decided to present a vegetarian alternative, with a spinach filling instead of the traditional lamb. Commonly these dumplings are cooked directly in the hot yoghurt, but I find that baking them first lets them hold their shape better and give a pleasing crunch with every bite.

Don't let yourself – or your family – snack on the baked dumplings beforehand, otherwise you'll soon be popping one after another and end up with nothing but a hot garlicky yoghurt stew.

To make the filling, wash and dry the spinach, then chop it finely and rub with the salt. Place in a colander set over a bowl and firmly squeeze the spinach, reserving the juices in the bowl. Put the spinach leaves into a separate bowl and mix with the onion, cinnamon and allspice. Set aside to marinate while you prepare the dough.

Prepare the dough by rubbing the oil into the flour. Add the sugar, if using, and 150 ml (scant ⅔ cup) of the reserved spinach juice. Mix well, then knead until a dough is formed. Cover and leave to rest for 20 minutes.

Meanwhile, preheat the oven to 200°C (400°F/gas 6).

Divide the dough into thirds. On a floured work surface, roll out a piece to 2 mm (1/16 in) thick (keeping the other pieces covered). Use a 7 cm (3 in) cookie cutter or the top of a small glass to cut the dough into circles.

Fill each circle of dough with about ½ teaspoon of the spinach filling,

For the filling
500 g (1 lb 2 oz) spinach
1 tablespoon sea salt
150 g (5 oz) onion, finely chopped
1 teaspoon cinnamon
1 teaspoon allspice

For the dough
2 tablespoons olive oil, plus extra for brushing
300 g (2 cups) plain (all-purpose) flour, plus extra for dusting
2½ teaspoons sugar (optional)

For the sauce
100 g (scant ½ cup) short-grain rice
1.2 kg (4¾ cups) plain yoghurt
500 ml (2 cups) water
2 tablespoons cornflour (cornstarch)
3 teaspoons salt
2 garlic cloves
1 tablespoon dried mint

Basic Pilaf (page 208), to serve (optional)

MAINS 134

fold in half to make a half-moon shape and pinch the edges to seal, making sure no filling is oozing out. Overlap and pinch together the two tips underneath the dumpling. Place on an oiled baking tray and brush the tops with oil. Repeat until all the dough and filling is used up.

To make the sauce, soak the rice in water for about 15 minutes. Mix together the yoghurt, water, cornflour and 2 teaspoons of the salt in a large saucepan. Bring to the boil, stirring to avoid lumps forming. Once it boils, drain the rice, add to the pan and stir – this prevents the rice from sinking to the bottom of the pan and burning. Reduce the heat and cook for about 15 minutes or so, stirring occasionally, until the rice is cooked and the yoghurt has thickened.

Meanwhile, bake the dumplings for 10–15 minutes until lightly golden on top.

Pound the garlic in a pestle and mortar with the remaining 1 teaspoon of salt until creamy. Add to the yoghurt sauce along with the dried mint and stir.

If you like, you can drop the dumplings into the yoghurt sauce and allow it to come back to the boil before serving. Alternatively, serve the hot dumplings with the sauce on the side. It can also be served with rice pilaf.

TARO ROOT WITH CHICKPEAS
Qolqas bi Hummus

The Christians of Beirut prepare this vegetarian dish during Lent, which coincides with the availability of plenty of seasonal vegetables. This recipe is also common in Minieh in North Lebanon, and is one of of the few fading recipes that still use taro – a much-neglected vegetable. Taro is a root vegetable that produces a sticky substance when peeled that will numb your tongue if consumed untreated. The old way of preparing it was to cube it and leave it to dry in the sun for a couple of days, but now we fry it and that removes the unwanted sensation. It is only in season here during the colder months, making this a favourite winter dish.

Heat an 8 cm (3 in) depth of vegetable oil in a deep-fryer or deep heavy-based saucepan to 180°C (350°F).

Meanwhile, with a sharp knife, peel and cut the taro root into large cubes.

Deep-fry the taro root in batches in the hot oil until golden. Remove with a slotted spoon to drain on paper towels.

Heat the olive oil in a large saucepan over a medium-high heat, add the onion and sauté until golden. Add the chickpeas, salt and water and bring to the boil, then add the fried taro root, reduce the heat and simmer, covered, for 20 minutes until slightly thickened.

Season with lemon juice and taste to adjust the seasoning.

Serve with a plate of fresh mint, radishes, spring onions, cucumbers and olives, with some soft pita bread for scooping.

vegetable oil, for deep-frying

1.6 kg (3 lb 8 oz) taro root

60 ml (¼ cup) olive oil

400 g (14 oz) onion, finely chopped

400 g (14 oz) tinned chickpeas (garbanzo beans), drained

1 tablespoon salt

1 litre (4 cups) water

60 ml (¾ cup) lemon juice

To serve

fresh mint leaves

radishes

spring onions (scallions)

cucumbers

olives

soft pita bread

LENTIL PILAF WITH CARAMELISED ONIONS
Mjaddara Hamra

500 g (1 lb 2 oz) whole red lentils, rinsed

2.25 litres (9 cups) water

600 g (1 lb 5 oz) onions, finely chopped

120 ml (½ cup) olive oil

150 g (scant 1 cup) coarse bulgur wheat

2 teaspoons salt, or to taste

To serve (optional – you choose)

soft Arabic bread or markouk/saj bread,
for scooping

Zesty Cabbage Salad (page 82)

Fattoush (page 80)

fresh veggies and herbs

pickled chillies

green olives

One of the dishes that always causes a dispute is *mjaddara*. There are so many variations to the recipe, but the uniting elements are lentils, onions, and bulgur or rice. The debates range from which lentils are used and are they creamed, to whether you use bulgur or rice or spices and is it *mjaddara* or *mdardara*? The list goes on... To me, *mjaddara* is when the proportions of lentils to bulgur/rice is higher. *Mdardara* uses almost equal proportions and is flavoured with cumin and fried onions on top. *Mjaddara safra* uses split yellow lentils; *mjaddara hamra* uses whole ones and gets its flavour from deeply caramelising the onions. *Msaffaye* means 'strained' and is made by pureeing cooked brown lentils, then cooking the rice or bulgur with them until thickened. A recipe in *Kitab al-Tabikh*, a cookbook compiled in 1226 by al-Baghdadi in Iraq, stated that this beloved vegetarian dish was served with minced (ground) meat in rich people's celebrations, while the meatless one was the food of the poor.

Mjaddara hamra is what my family used to make. It is common in South Lebanon and Palestine. My grandma called it the 'nails of the knees' because of the high iron content. Pair it with some fresh bread, a zesty salad, green olives and lots of fresh veggies.

Add the lentils to a large saucepan, cover with 2 litres (8 cups) of the water and bring to the boil, then reduce the heat and simmer for 30 minutes.

Place the onions in a cold sauté pan with the olive oil, set over a medium–high heat and fry until they start to caramelise. Stir often to make sure they are browning evenly, and keep them on the heat until they turn from caramelised to very dark brown – almost but not quite charring. The burnt onions are what gives this dish its special flavour. Once the onions reach this stage, add the extra cup of water and bring to the boil.

Pour the onion mixture into the cooked lentils, then stir in the bulgur. Season to taste with the salt. Bring to the boil and cook for a further 5 minutes, stirring often, until the bulgur has soaked up the extra liquid.

Ladle onto plates and let cool slightly before serving with your chosen accompaniments. I love to scoop this dish up with soft Arabic bread.

LENTIL STEW WITH HOME-MADE NOODLES
Rishta bi Adas

Rishta is a winter dish, mostly known in the villages of the Lebanon. The first time I tasted it, it had been made by the mother of a crush of mine. It reminded me of a lemony lentil and chard soup but with noodles. It wasn't the best thing I'd had, but then neither was the crush! Many heartbreaks later, a Syrian version of this dish called *horaa osbao* came up from Dima, a friend who is originally from Damascus, at one of our gatherings. It was delicious comfort food – a flavour festival. Here, I've combined elements from the traditional Lebanese recipe with Dima's version – to take it even closer to the Syrian dish you could also garnish it with fried bread and pomegranate seeds. If you like, you can use 250 g (9 oz) of ready-made tagliatelle rather than making noodles from scratch.

First, make the noodle dough. In a large bowl, mix together the flour and salt, then gradually add the water (depending on your flour, you may need a little less water) and knead until a firm dough forms. Knead a little longer until the dough is soft and smooth. Cover and leave to rest for 10 minutes.

Combine the lentils and water in a saucepan and bring to the boil, then reduce the heat and simmer for 15 minutes or until the lentils are soft.

Meanwhile, heat 2 tablespoons of the olive oil in a frying pan (skillet) over a medium heat. Add the onions and fry, stirring occasionally, until just starting to lightly brown. Stop the cooking with 2 tablespoons of water, then add the onions to the lentil pan.

Divide the dough and roll out on a floured work surface into very thin strips (or use a pasta machine). Cut with a roller cutter or knife into thin noodles, sprinkle with a little more flour and toss to coat. Repeat to use up all of the dough. Shake off the excess flour and drop the noodles into the cooked lentils. Stir and leave to cook for 2–3 minutes.

Meanwhile, heat the remaining 1 tablespoon of olive oil in the same pan you used to cook the onions and sauté the pesto until fragrant. Stir in the lemon zest and juice and remove from the heat. Add the mixture to the lentils and noodles, then remove the pan from the heat.

Serve in bowls, scattered with fresh coriander leaves, with lemon wedges for squeezing over and plenty of pomegranate molasses for drizzling.

For the noodle dough
200 g (1⅔ cups) plain (all-purpose) flour, plus extra for dusting

½ teaspoon fine salt

up to 150 ml (scant ⅔ cup) water

For the stew
350 g (scant 1½ cups) whole brown or red lentils, rinsed

2 litres (8 cups) water

3 tablespoons olive oil

250 g (9 oz) onions, thinly sliced

2 tablespoons Coriander and Garlic Pesto (page 209)

zest of 1 lemon, plus 150 ml (scant ⅔ cup) lemon juice

To serve
handful of coriander (cilantro) leaves

lemon wedges, for squeezing

pomegranate molasses, for drizzling

BUTTER BEANS WITH LEMONY GARLIC DRESSING
Fasoulya Areeda Mtabbale

300 g (2 cups) dried butter (lima) beans
or 800 g (1 lb 12 oz) tinned/jarred

3 garlic cloves

½ teaspoon sea salt

120 ml (½ cup) olive oil

zest of 1 lemon, plus 75 ml
(5 tablespoons) lemon juice

handful of flat-leaf parsley

Whether you're serving this dish as a main, a side or a salad, you'll fall in love with it. Fat creamy beans and zesty lemony garlic dressing and loads of good olive oil! Prepare it in advance and let it bathe in all the delicious juices. Try it scooped up in Arabic bread or on a good toasted slice of sourdough.

This is my favourite way to have butter (lima) beans. In season, you find them fresh – or green, as we call them – in produce shops and supermarkets here in the Lebanon. Out of season, the dried ones work just fine when soaked and cooked. This recipe can be prepared with other white beans, but you'll be missing out on the flavour and creaminess of these delicious beans.

If using the dried beans, soak them overnight in plenty of water.

The next day, drain the beans, place in a saucepan and cover with fresh water. Bring to the boil, then reduce the heat and simmer for about 30 minutes until cooked. Alternatively, pour the jarred or tinned beans into a saucepan and gently reheat.

Pound the garlic in a pestle and mortar with the salt until creamy, then slowly add the olive oil and stir until it becomes a thick sauce. Slowly pour in the lemon juice while stirring to combine.

Drain the beans, if necessary, and season with the lemony garlic dressing, lemon zest and chopped parsley and serve.

SUNDAY FEAST

We Lebanese can find a thousand and one things to divide ourselves over, but despite all our differences, there are two common points we can all agree on: we love food and we love a traditional gathering.

On Sundays, almost every family arranges a food-filled lunch gathering with close or extended family. A few of my own favourite family gatherings that come to mind have been held at the country house of my mom's maternal uncle, Khalo Fahd. The wood-fired pot filled with thick-cut potatoes to be fried until perfectly crisp; the grill hot and ready for the meats; salads and dips tantalise until the meats are ready, with platters of vegetables, olives and pickles to nibble on. The table spread always as appetising to the eye as to the palate: simple yet beautiful, with mismatched plates and forks laid on a newspaper 'tablecloth'. Khalo Fahd's late wife Beba would entertain everyone as we all helped with the preparations.

Meat always expresses a special celebration: the return of a loved one from abroad, a wedding, a graduation, a long-awaited gathering, and so on. Once the sacrificial animal is slaughtered, all parts of it must be used, and there is a recipe to savour and feast on every part. On the day of the slaughter, men often compete for the lungs, heart, liver and kidneys, eating them raw with a glass of *arak*, as they believe the alcohol kills any germs or microbes the meat might have. For those of us who

don't want to try this, there are delicious traybakes or pilafs, stretched with rice or burghul or vegetables, with vibrant and fresh side dishes.

Gatherings here are not constricted by eating time. A Sunday feast can start at midday and extend until sunset, even in the longer days of summer. First, we nibble on seasonal produce: pickles and green olives and soaked almonds in autumn, and fresh veggies, such as green almonds, peas and fresh broad-bean (fava-bean) pods, from early spring to summer. Salads and dips reach the table while the main meal is being cooked. The serving of the main dish is a ceremonial act in itself, performed by the host. Grilled meats are placed on a tray in between loaves of bread to keep them warm and soak up the juices and the host carefully sends skewers across the table especially to the shy guests. The same is done if it's a traybake or a dish served in one large serving plate. Sometimes it's considered rude to refuse and can suggest that the guest is not comfortable or the food is not up to their liking. (You'd never be able to say no to a second serving from the hands of Khalo Fahd.) The savoury part of the meal can extend to over an an hour or two in some households, based on the conversation and the harmony of those around the table. Then come the fruit and desserts, which can be another hour, as we slowly grab fruits to peel and share or accept sweets that we really can't reject, followed by cups of bitter coffee and a view of the sunset or a walk and a chat among the olive trees. I wouldn't trade it for the world.

Typically, lunches are the main meal for people. Even now, with the dynamics changing to 8-to-5 jobs, lunch is still the main event. Dinners are usually a little lighter, especially if had at home. In this chapter, a few *centre-de-table* dishes are presented for the Sunday feast, but any of the recipes in the Mains chapter would work as well.

FREEKEH PILAF WITH BEEF & CHICKEN
Freekeh a'a Djej

I can't think of a more appropriate dish for a gathering. This pilaf is commonly served spread over a large dish with the chicken arranged on top and garnished with lots of fried nuts (my favourite part). It makes a great centrepiece and is perfect for a regular family meal, for large gatherings or for special occasions, such as Easter Sunday.

This recipe is commonly known as *riz a'a djej* (rice on chicken), but some make it with freekeh instead of rice and cubed meat instead of minced. You can make it as you like – either way, it will be a favourite. Serve with a side of plain yoghurt, or a refreshing salad, or a simple gravy made with the extra chicken stock from poaching the chicken.

Put the whole chicken, vegetables, spices and salt into a large stockpot and add enough water to cover. Bring to the boil and remove the foam that rises to the top, then reduce the heat, cover and simmer for 1 hour.

Allow to cool slightly, then remove the chicken and divide into large pieces, keeping the skin on. Set aside. Strain the stock, discarding the vegetables and spices, and set aside.

For the pilaf, heat the oil in a large saucepan over a medium heat, add the beef, spices and salt, and sauté until the meat is browned. Add the freekeh and sauté for 1–2 minutes, then pour over 1.2 litres (4¾ cups) of the chicken stock (if using rice, you may only need 750 ml/3 cups). Stir well, bring to the boil, then reduce the heat, cover, and simmer for 30 minutes (20 minutes for rice) until the liquid is absorbed. Once done, remove from the heat and fluff with a fork, then cover and leave to rest for 5 minutes.

Meanwhile, make the garnish. Heat the olive oil and butter, if using, in a small frying pan (skillet) over a medium heat and fry the nuts until golden and fragrant. Remove to drain on paper towels.

Heat the grill (broiler) to high and grill the chicken pieces until the skin is browned and crispy. If you prefer, you can remove the bones from the meat before grilling. Alternatively, shred the chicken into bite-sized chunks.

Spread the pilaf over a large serving plate, top with the chicken pieces or shredded meat and sprinkle with the fried nuts.

For the poached chicken
1 x whole chicken (1.6 kg/3 lb 8 oz)

2 onions, halved

1 carrot, halved

pared zest of ½ lemon

1 cinnamon stick

2 bay leaves

¼ whole nutmeg, or a few gratings

2 cardamom pods

1 tablespoon salt

For the beef pilaf
2 tablespoons olive oil

200 g (7 oz) minced (ground) beef

¼ teaspoon ground nutmeg

1 teaspoon allspice

½ teaspoon ground cinnamon

1 teaspoon salt

400 g (2 cups) freekeh (or long-grain rice), rinsed

To garnish
1 tablespoon olive oil

1 tablespoon butter (optional)

40 g (½ cup) almonds (halved or slivered/flaked)

40 g (⅓ cup) cashews

20 g (2½ tablespoons) pine nuts

GRILLED CHICKEN SHISH KEBAB
Shish Taouk

In addition to being a very popular sandwich and a quick street food, *shish taouk* is a must-have for a barbecue gathering, be it for a casual affair, a big Sunday feast, or a humble camping trip.

The kebab mixture can be prepared ahead of time (overnight is best, if possible) and can even be frozen, then thawed when needed. The secret is in the spice marinade – it brings a rounded, distinctive flavour that is unique to the *taouk* you can buy anywhere in Lebanon. I love it with some extra lemon as I find it goes well with the *toom* and pickles. Some people prefer to add yoghurt to the marinade and that works to tenderise the chicken breasts and help give them colour when grilled. I prefer this dairy-free version that we make at home. This is my mom's much-used recipe and there is a sort of comfort in the taste of it for me.

If you're using wooden skewers to cook with, soak them overnight in water to prevent burning.

Place the chicken in a bowl with all of the other ingredients and mix well. Cover and marinate overnight in the refrigerator.

The next day, prepare a charcoal grill or preheat a grill pan to high.

Cut your chosen vegetables into similar bite-sized cubes.

Arrange the chicken and veggies on skewers and brush with a little oil. Grill the skewers over charcoal for a smoky flavour, or on the grill pan, turning them frequently until cooked through.

Serve with *toom* or hummus, or both, and French fries, in pita or flatbreads if you like.

Pictured overleaf.

1 kg (2 lb 4 oz) skinless chicken breast, cut into bite-sized chunks

¼ teaspoon white pepper

⅛ teaspoon ground cardamom

⅛ teaspoon ground nutmeg

1 tablespoon paprika

1 teaspoon chilli powder

1 teaspoon salt

1 garlic clove, minced

20 g (¾ oz) fresh root ginger, minced

60 ml (¼ cup) olive oil, plus extra for brushing

zest of 1 lemon plus 1 tablespoon freshly squeezed lemon juice

2 tablespoons tomato paste

To serve

vegetables of choice: onions, mushrooms, bell peppers...

Toom (pages 68–71)

Hummus (pages 32–5)

French fries

thin flatbreads or pita bread

GRILLED KEBABS WITH PARSLEY & ONION SALAD
Kabab Meshwe w Biwaz

1 kg (2 lb 4 oz) minced (ground) beef

200 g (7 oz) minced (ground) lamb

250 g (9 oz) onions, grated

3 teaspoons salt

2 teaspoons allspice

1½ teaspoons ground nutmeg

50 g (3 heaped tablespoons) tomato paste

30 g (2 tablespoons) red pepper paste

olive oil, for brushing

For the *biwaz* salad

300 g (10½ oz) onions, thinly sliced

2 tablespoons sumac

small bunch of flat-leaf parsley, chopped

To serve

pita bread

red pepper paste, to taste

In English, mostly due to Ottoman and Persian influence on some dishes and their names, *kebab* or *kabob* means any skewered meat, whether it is cubes of meat or a huge rotating spit. But to us, *kabab* is a spiced meat mixture shaped on wide metal skewers and grilled over charcoal or wood.

I sound biased when I say my mom makes the best *kabab*, but I have a story to back this claim up (or that highlights my weak will or sense of commitment, you decide!). Despite being a butcher's son, I was a picky eater when it came to red meat – I wouldn't eat large pieces of meat unless they were almost charred and rubbery, or had been minced into meatballs, *kafta* or *kibbeh*. After an argument with my mom about how it's all meat regardless of the shape, I decided to quit eating it altogether. I caved only two years later when she was grilling her famous *kabab* one Sunday. She would wrap each *kabab* in wide strips of pita bread filled with spicy chilli paste and *biwaz* (sliced onions mixed with sumac and parsley), then grill them. It is *kabab* taken to a whole new level. I couldn't resist it then, two years after not a single bite of red meat, and I can't resist it now.

In a large bowl, mix together the beef, lamb, grated onions, salt, spices and pastes. Mix with your hands until incorporated, but avoid overworking the meat, otherwise the kebabs will be tough. Marinate for 1 hour or overnight.

Prepare a charcoal grill or preheat a grill pan to high.

Shape the kebab mixture into thick fingers or squeeze balls of the mixture onto oiled metal skewers. Shape by squeezing with your thumb and index finger, starting from the top and working down at 1 cm (½ in) intervals.

Grill the skewers over charcoal for a smoky flavour, or on the grill pan, turning them frequently until cooked through.

For the *biwaz*, rub the onions with the sumac, then mix with the parsley.

To serve, open a pita bread and slather a tablespoon of red pepper paste inside, then fill with a little of the *biwaz* mixture. Close the bread and grill slightly on both sides, then cut into triangles. Use the bread to wrap around the grilled kebabs for an incredible bite.

Pictured overleaf.

PEARL COUSCOUS & CARAWAY STEW WITH CHICKEN

Moghrabieh Lebneniye

The Levant is a melting pot (no pun intended) of cultures that passed through this land through history. Some recipes can be traced back thousands of years and some form of them is still being cooked in homes to this day. *Moghrabieh* can be traced back to Al Maghreb (Morocco), as the name suggests, and reveals how couscous used to be prepared by hand at home. Couscous evolved into the store-bought version everyone knows, but *moghrabieh* pearls are still prepared by hand by Palestinians and Palestinian Jordanians and those who learned from them.

When writing this recipe, I was torn between the Palestinian method I inherited from my family or the Lebanese version you will find in restaurants. The Palestinian version uses *maftoul*, an early form of hand-rolled couscous made with cracked wheat. The stew is based on a lamb-bone broth with chickpeas (garbanzo beans) and onions and is light on spices to highlight the lamb flavour. The Lebanese version, on the other hand, is prepared with store-bought *moghrabieh* pearls, usually with chicken and more spices, with pearl onions and chickpeas added to the broth. Each version is unique, but the most important feature, apart from the flavours, is how it gathers people around the table. We rarely prepare *moghrabieh* for a small lunch. It's always made for a feast with family and friends and we still get people asking to be invited the next time we cook it.

Start with the chicken. Heat the olive oil in a large pot over a medium heat, place the chicken in the pot and turn in the hot oil to brown on all sides. Add the cinnamon sticks, bay leaves, salt, lemon and onion and cover with the measured water. Bring to the boil and simmer for at least 1 hour, skimming off and discarding any foam if it rises.

If you are using moghrabieh that needs to be pre-steamed, top the broth pot with an oiled colander or steamer basket, add the moghrabieh and steam over the flavourful broth as it simmers for about 30 minutes. Cover with a clean dish towel (this will absorb the vapour instead of letting it drop back over the couscous) and the pan lid. Carefully break up the grains occasionally with a fork or skewer to prevent them sticking together.

For the poached chicken and broth

1 tablespoon olive oil

1 x 1.2 kg (2 lb 11 oz) chicken

2 cinnamon sticks

3 bay leaves

1 tablespoon salt, plus extra to taste

½ lemon

1 large onion, halved

2 litres (8 cups) water

For the stew

3 tablespoons olive oil, plus extra for greasing

500 g (1½ cups) moghrabieh pearl couscous (giant couscous)

500 g (1 lb 2 oz) pearl onions, peeled

2 x 400g (14 oz) tins chickpeas (garbanzo beans), drained

1 tablespoon ground caraway, or more to taste

1 tablespoon ground cinnamon, or more to taste

½ tablespoon allspice, or more to taste

1 tablespoon ground cumin, or more to taste

recipe continues overleaf...›

...> Take the chicken out of the broth and let it cool a little. Strain the broth and set aside. Portion the chicken into thighs, drumsticks and breasts but keep the skin on. Shred the rest of the meat remaining on the chicken and set aside. (If you like, before serving, you can grill (broil) the whole pieces until the skin browns and gets a little crispy.)

For the stew, heat 1 tablespoon of the oil in a large saucepan over a medium heat, add the pearl onions and leave them untouched until they start to brown a little, then flip and brown the other sides. Pour the reserved broth over the onions, then add the chickpeas and most of the spices. Bring to a simmer and cook for about 20 minutes until the onions have softened. Taste and adjust the spicing, if needed.

In a separate saucepan, heat the remaining oil over a medium heat. Stir in the moghrabieh until well coated, then add the remaining spices and stir carefully, making sure not to break the moghrabieh, until fragrant. Gradually add ½ cup of the simmering broth and toss until it has been absorbed.

Once the onions in the broth are cooked, add the shredded chicken and the spiced moghrabieh and stir until they start absorbing some of the liquid and the stew begins to thicken. The stew should be quite saucy, so don't let the broth be fully absorbed by the moghrabieh. Add more broth, if needed. Turn off the heat and transfer the stew to a serving bowl. Top with the chicken pieces and serve immediately.

PUMPKIN KIBBEH
Kibbet Laqtin

I can't think of any other traditional use for pumpkin in Lebanon than the *kibbeh*, that's either formed into the familiar balls or baked in a tray with a delicious and nutritious filling that will certainly keep you from asking for meat. During Lent, Christians abstain from having any type of meat, and some adopt a strictly vegan diet. Pumpkin *kibbeh* balls are prepared in some Christian villages on Good Friday. They call it *Kibbet El Haziné* (the *kibbeh* of those who are sad), in reference to the sorrowful memorial of Christ's crucifixion. The traybake makes for a great main dish, especially for a vegan or vegetarian feast, or a good side dish for a sharing table.

Preheat the oven to 180°C (350°F/gas 4).

In a large bowl, combine the cooked pumpkin with the bulgur, onion, herbs, spices and salt. Mix with your hands until everything is well combined. Add the flour very gradually until the dough firms up but is not tough – you may not need it all.

For the filling, heat 2 tablespoons of the olive oil in a frying pan (skillet) over a medium heat, add the onions and salt and sauté until softened. Gradually add the spinach or chard and cook until wilted and all the water has evaporated. Remove from the heat and mix in the sumac and chopped walnuts. Leave to cool.

Grease a 24 cm (10 in) deep-sided baking pan with oil. Spread half of the pumpkin *kibbeh* mixture in an even layer in the pan, top with the cooled filling mixture and cover with the rest of the *kibbeh* mixture. To make this process easier, shape small amounts of the *kibbeh* into patties and use them to evenly cover the filling. Press the *kibbeh* with the heels of your palms to pack it tightly, then poke a hole in the middle with your finger or the end of a wooden spoon. Use a sharp knife to cut the *kibbeh* into 6–8 pieces and score the pieces with a geometric pattern of your choice. Scoring it will help to create more crispy bits on the top. Pour the remaining olive oil down the hole you made, allowing it to overflow. Tilt the tray and make sure all of the surface of the *kibbeh* has been covered with the oil.

Bake for 30–35 minutes until it has shrunk around the sides and lightly browned on top.

Serve with a zesty cabbage or cucumber and yoghurt salad, or *tabbouleh*.

For the pumpkin *kibbeh* mixture

600 g (1 lb 5 oz) cooked pumpkin (or 1 kg/2 lb 4 oz raw pumpkin, peeled, then roasted)

400 g (2⅓ cups) fine whole-wheat bulgur wheat, rinsed and drained

50 g (2 oz) onions, grated

8 basil leaves, finely chopped

2 sprigs of mint, finely chopped

2 sprigs of marjoram, finely chopped

1 teaspoon allspice

½ teaspoon ground nutmeg

2 teaspoons salt

75–120 g (½–¾ cup) plain (all-purpose) flour

For the filling

60 ml (¼ cup) olive oil, plus extra for greasing

600 g (1 lb 5 oz) onions, thinly sliced

1 teaspoon salt

500 g (1 lb 2 oz) spinach or Swiss chard, thinly sliced

2 tablespoons sumac

150 g (1½ cups) finely chopped walnuts

To serve

Cucumber and Yoghurt Salad (page 81) or Zesty Cabbage Salad (page 82) or *Tabbouleh* (page 78)

DESSERTS

Lebanese sweets are legendary and, like most foods in the region, claiming ownership over one or another is a bit absurd. There are numerous versions of sweet dishes from different regions. And then there are some regions that are well known for particular things they do well. I've selected here a few simple desserts and some that need a little more work (and some elbow grease!) to achieve, but mostly I wanted to document and share a few little-known sweet recipes, even to people who live in Beirut.

Desserts, as well as being an integral part of the *asrouniyeh* ritual (afternoon tea, see page 166), will always finish off a Lebanese meal. Sometimes, as soon as food plates are taken off the table, dessert is laid down, along with fruit platters and coffee. I actually prefer to take my time, cleanse my palate, then enjoy dessert as a standalone dish.

But who says dessert is only for after lunch or dinner? We have *knafeh* for breakfast, which is a white oozy cheese baked with a semolina crust, stuffed into a sesame bun and doused with syrup. It's rather like having a sweet meat- and veg-less burger for breakfast!

Some of my favourite desserts to eat while out and about in Beirut are the ice creams and sorbets from Mitri, the Beirut ice-cream vendor who has been featured numerous times in international media (see pages 183–5) and whose wares almost need no introduction. His humble shop is a must-visit destination if you are in the city.

SEMOLINA & COCONUT CAKE
Nammoura

Nammoura is a fudgy, moist coconut cake with semolina and yoghurt as a base. There are a couple of recipes for it in my mom's old recipe book, but I asked her for the easiest and most fail-safe one and here it is. The prepared batter looks very runny before baking, but the semolina absorbs the liquid and it bakes into a fine, soft cake. Don't be afraid of the syrup quantity. The cake will absorb it and it creates the essential *nammoura* texture without being overly and sickeningly sweet. My mom couldn't let go of the fact that I used half of the syrup in the first testing, so don't make the same mistake – otherwise she'll judge you too!

Preheat the oven to 180°C (350°F/gas 4).

Toast the coconut in a pan or on a baking sheet in the oven until golden.

In a large bowl, rub the oil into the semolina until well coated. Add the toasted coconut, yoghurt, sugar, salt and baking powder and mix well. The mixture is supposed to be quite wet and runny, so adjust the mixture depending on the thickness of your yoghurt.

Brush a 23-cm (9-in) square, deep-sided baking pan with a little tahini to prevent sticking and pour the batter into it. Lightly score the top of the batter into squares or diamonds and place an almond half in the middle of each section. Bake for 20–25 minutes until the sides are browned and pulling away from the pan – that means the bottom is done.

Meanwhile, preheat the grill (broiler) to high.

Transfer the pan to the grill for 5 minutes until the top is golden.

Meanwhile, prepare the syrup by mixing the water, sugar, lemon juice and rose geranium leaves, if using, in a saucepan over a medium heat, stirring until the sugar has dissolved. Boil for 5 minutes, then remove from the heat and stir in the rose water and orange blossom water.

As soon as it comes out of the oven, douse the *nammoura* with all of the syrup. It might seem like a lot, but trust me – the cake will soak it all up when it is hot. Allow it to cool a little, then cut into the pre-scored sections and allow to cool completely before serving.

40 g (½ cup) dried shredded (desiccated) or freshly grated coconut

120 ml (½ cup) vegetable oil

300 g (2 cups) coarse semolina

400–500 g (1⅔–2 cups) plain yoghurt

230 g (1 cup) caster (superfine) sugar

¼ teaspoon salt

1 teaspoon baking powder

tahini, for brushing the pan

32 blanched almond halves

For the syrup

375 ml (1½ cups) water

450 g (2 cups) caster (superfine) sugar

1 tsp lemon juice

handful of rose geranium leaves (if available)

2 tbsp rose water

2 tbsp orange blossom water

SWEET SEMOLINA COOKIES WITH ASHTA
Ma'amoul Madd Ashta

300 g (2 cups) coarse semolina

150 g (1 cup) plain (all-purpose) flour

75 g (⅓ cup) caster (superfine) sugar

150 g (scant ⅔ cup) butter or ghee, softened

2 teaspoons baking powder

¼ teaspoon dried yeast

½ teaspoon fine salt

75 ml (5 tablespoons) milk

For the filling

1 x recipe quantity of *Ashta* (page 219)

For the syrup

350 g (1½ cups) caster (superfine) sugar

175 ml (¾ cup) water

handful of rose geranium leaves (if available)

1 tablespoon rose water

1 tablespoon orange blossom water

To serve

orange blossom petal jam

ground pistachios

Ma'amoul is the stuffed semolina cookie prepared during Easter and Fitr holidays. But *ma'amoul madd*, which translates to 'spread-out' or 'sheet cookie', is found almost all year round. The ingredients are similar but the texture is different. While regular *ma'amoul* are baked to a light golden hue and are usually dry and crumbly, these reach a beautiful caramel colour and are doused in simple syrup to give them their sweet flavour. The *ashta*-filled ones are highly prized. Try using the *Baklava* filling (page 178) too, possibly replacing the walnuts with pistachios or cashews.

Mix the semolina, flour and sugar in a bowl. Add the softened butter or ghee and rub in until incorporated. Cover and set aside for 1 hour, or overnight in the refrigerator, to allow the flours to absorb the fat.

When ready to cook, preheat the oven to 200°C (400°F/gas 6).

Mix the baking powder, yeast and salt into the semolina mixture, then gradually stir in the milk until a dough is formed. It is ready when you can squeeze a handful together and it will hold its shape. Divide the dough in half. Press one half in an even layer into the bottom of a 23-cm (9-in) square, deep-sided baking pan. Top with the *ashta*, spreading it over evenly.

Place the other half of the dough on a sheet of clingfilm (plastic wrap) or baking paper and roll out with a rolling pin to the size of the baking pan. Use the clingfilm/paper to help flip or slide it over the *ashta* layer. This is tricky as it breaks easily, so go gently. Tap into place until all of the *ashta* is covered.

Bake for 20–25 minutes until the sides are golden.

To make the syrup, mix the sugar, water and rose geranium, if using, in a pan over a medium heat. Stir until the sugar is dissolved. Boil for 5 minutes, then remove from the heat and stir in the rose and orange blossom waters.

Meanwhile, heat the grill (broiler) to high. Transfer the baking pan to the grill for 5 minutes until the top of the *ma'amoul* is golden.

As soon as it is baked, douse the top of the *ma'amoul* with the syrup and leave it to absorb all the liquid. Let it cool completely, then cut and serve with orange blossom petal jam and ground pistachios sprinkled on top.

AFTERNOON TEA

Asrouniyeh

There is a custom that is fading in modern life, mostly due to long working hours and busy schedules. Workers used to work from the early hours of the day then come back home for a late lunch and an afternoon siesta. They'd wake up to cups of strong Lebanese coffee, sometimes flavoured with cardamom, and an assortment of small sweet or savoury dishes. The custom was named for the time of the day: dusk or *a'asr*. Thus, *asrouniyeh*.

I have vivid memories of times spent at my aunt's house, or the frequent visits from my mom's uncle: whether we spent the day picking olives or playing around with the chickens and ducks or simply having one of those extended lunches, we'd eventually situate ourselves under an olive tree a couple of hours before sunset, or under the huge mulberry tree that stretched its branches wider than their house itself. We'd plate up a few pieces of *nammoura* or *ma'amoul* or maybe a few bites of bitter orange preserve or some bread and jam.

One of my favourite snacks is a dip, unique for its rich flavour and sweet and savoury notes: carob molasses and tahini. We mix it in a one-to-one ratio and dip bread into it. It is rich and chocolatey with no added sugar and it sure is satisfying. Another super-simple snack consists of mastic-flavoured *lokum*, or *Rahet El Halkoum*, crushed between two Marie biscuits. These sweets go so well with sips of coffee (they are the reason I prefer my coffee with no sugar) or a cup of tea with a couple of stems of rose geranium, which is how my mom makes it.

Along with all the sweet snacks, the classic savoury bite is *Ka'ak Asrouniye* (pages 56–9) – its name perfectly fitting for the time of the day. The typical filling for the purse-shaped bread is a drizzle of olive oil and a dash of za'atar or sumac, or maybe a triangle of *Picon* (processed cheese).

On hotter days, *asrouniyeh* takes a fresher turn. A tall glass of mulberry, bitter orange or rose syrup drink will quench your thirst and cool you down. Warm desserts are replaced with ice cream or fresh seasonal fruits. Summer is generous with plenty of stone fruits and refreshing watermelon. We're never out of options.

So, find a spot in the shade, a place with a fine breeze to place a few small wooden chairs with straw seats, to drink glasses of refreshing cordial and snack on plates of goodies. Call it our tea-time tradition.

CARAWAY-SPICED PUDDING
Meghli

Meghli is typically presented to guests who visit to congratulate a family on a birth. It it one of the traditions that has stood the test of time. The spices in this pudding are warm and, to me, they're comforting. Mom makes it every Christmas for the birth of Jesus and she even made some when our cat gave birth to six baby kittens.

I love this pudding served at room temperature with lots of coconut and nuts decorating the top, but you can use your favourite selection of dried fruits and nuts or whatever's available.

Ahead of serving, soak the nuts and sultanas individually in water for 2 hours, then drain.

Pour the water into a small saucepan, then whisk in the rice flour, spices and sugar until incorporated. Bring to the boil, stirring constantly until it thickens.

Divide the mixture among 4–6 glass bowls and sprinkle with shredded coconut to cover the surface and prevent a skin forming. Serve warm or allow it to come to room temperature before covering and refrigerating.

Decorate the bowls with the nuts and fruit just before serving.

1 litre (4 cups) water

150 g (generous ¾ cup) rice flour

1½ tablespoons ground caraway

1½ tablespoons ground cinnamon

120 g (½ cup) caster (superfine) sugar

To decorate

handful of dried shredded (desiccated) or freshly grated coconut

handful of blanched, skinned or nibbed pistachios

handful of blanched, skinned almonds

handful of walnuts

handful of pine nuts

handful of sultanas (golden raisins)

TURMERIC & TAHINI RICE PUDDING
Mfatta'a

As part of my mission to document fading Beiruti recipes, I was keen to try this. Hardly anyone knows about it, except for a few original Beirutis or those who grew up around the handful of shops or people who still make it. It is commonly prepared for the occasion of Job's (Ayoub) Wednesday, a day in April that's usually around the same time as Easter or Spring Equinox. The people of Ras Beirut, typically led by women, would march from their homes to Ramlet El Bayda beach to wash their bodies in the sea as a form of blessing. The tradition goes that the prophet Job was asked to swim in the sea to relieve the 40-year-long ailments inflicted on him by God to test his faith. People would bring seasonal foods to the beach gathering and would make *mfatta'a* specifically for the occasion.

Making it is a group effort and a test of patience. It certainly takes Job's patience to get through it and many hours to cook out the moisture from the tahini, sugar and rice. So, get together with some friends and find some elbow grease to make it. Traditionally, the thick pudding is spread into a thin layer, but you can shape it into balls for easier serving.

Soak the rice in 500 ml (2 cups) of the water for at least 1 hour, or overnight, then transfer to a saucepan, stir in the turmeric and the remaining water and bring to the boil. Reduce the heat, cover, and simmer for 30 minutes, or until most of the water is absorbed and rice is almost falling apart.

Remove from the heat and stir in the sugar and tahini until thoroughly combined. Return the pan to a medium heat and cook for at least 1 hour (even up to 2 hours), stirring. You're basically cooking off all of the water here, so you do need to keep moving the mixture around to allow it to cook properly. In the beginning, you can skip a minute or two of stirring and come back to it, but after 30 minutes you need to constantly move the mixture around until the oil from the tahini breaks out of the mix. Once that happens, mix in the pine nuts and remove from the heat to cool.

To serve, you can either divide it among small plates and decorate by pressing into it with the back of a spoon to make a pattern, or you can roll small scoops of the mixture into bite-sized balls. Store them covered or in an airtight container for up to 3 days or for up to a week in the refrigerator.

300 g (1⅓ cups) short-grain rice

1 litre (4 cups) water

30 g (4 tablespoons) ground turmeric

250 g (1 generous cup) caster (superfine) sugar

300 g (1 generous cup) tahini

30 g (3 tablespoons) pine nuts

LAYERED MILK & ORANGE PUDDING
Ashtaliye

vegetable oil, for greasing

500 ml (2 cups) orange juice

70 g (generous ½ cup) cornflour (cornstarch)

1 tablespoon orange blossom water

4 tablespoons caster (superfine) sugar

1 g (¼ teaspoon) mastic (optional) (found in Middle Eastern grocers or online)

500 ml (2 cups) milk

1 tablespoon rose water

To decorate
ground pistachios

dried rose petals

To serve
simple syrup (optional)

Ashtaliye and *mhallabiye* are terms usually used interchangeably for a milk pudding dessert. But only recently did I find out that *mhallabiye* is used for a soft pudding chilled in cups or small bowls, while *ashtaliye* (or *hetaliye* in Syrian and Palestinian, as my grandma used to call it) is chilled in a large tray and cut into cubes and served in small bowls with syrup to sweeten. I decided to borrow the habit of making a fruit pudding or jam layer from the *mhallabiye* and use it in this recipe, pouring it into a loaf pan to create a nicer shape. I used orange juice for the fruit layer, but you can use other fruit juices instead. Taste your orange juice before using it – if it is not sweet, you'll need to add a little sugar at the beginning of cooking to sweeten.

Lightly oil a 900 g (2 lb) loaf pan and set aside.

In a small saucepan, whisk together the orange juice and half of the cornflour until incorporated. Bring to the boil over a medium heat, stirring constantly until thickened. Remove from the heat and stir in the orange blossom water. Pour into the prepared loaf pan and spread evenly, then set aside to cool slightly.

In a pestle and mortar, pound the sugar and mastic to a powder.

Clean the saucepan and pour in the milk. Add the mastic and sugar powder along with the remaining cornflour and whisk until incorporated. Bring to the boil over a medium heat, stirring constantly until thickened. Remove from the heat and stir in the rose water.

Carefully pour the milk mixture over the cooled orange layer in the loaf pan. Pouring the mixture over the back of a spoon helps to prevent it from breaking the barely set surface.

Allow to cool to room temperature, then cover and refrigerate for at least 4 hours or overnight until completely set.

Before serving, run a knife around the edges of the pan to loosen the pudding. Place a serving plate over the pan and flip it carefully to turn out. Sprinkle the top with ground pistachios and dried rose petals. Slice and serve with some simple syrup, if needed.

APRICOT-LEATHER PUDDING
Na'ou'

Despite their differences, religious people have many things in common – practices and habits in particular. In both Christianity and Islam, fasting is common. Apart from religious reasons, some people also believe in the healing power of fasting. And with this common practice comes the foods traditionally consumed to break fast. *Na'ou'* is one of those traditional foods that people continue making without thinking too much about the reason it is for. During Lent, Christians consume it to break the fast, as the water and natural sugars from the apricots and fats from the nuts are very nutritious and will nourish the body after a long period of abstinence. In Islam, it is also advised to consume water, soup and a date or two before having a proper meal after breaking fast.

Another version of this pudding uses no cornflour and is thinned out into a drink rather than a pudding with the same nuts and dried fruits. Egyptians call it *Khsheif*. While in Beirut, *Khshief* is a sweet pomegranate salad with sugar, orange blossom water and nuts.

Snip or chop the apricot leather into large pieces – this helps it to break down more easily. Put the pieces into a bowl and pour the boiling water over them. Leave to soak for 4 hours or overnight.

If the mix is still chunky after this time, blitz it in a blender to make it smooth. Pour the mixture into a saucepan, add the sugar and cornflour and whisk to combine. Place over a medium heat and bring to the boil, stirring constantly to avoid clumping, until the mixture thickens slightly.

Remove from the heat and let cool a little, then add the orange blossom water and rose water and leave to cool completely.

Meanwhile, chop the dried apricots and prunes and soak in enough hot water to barely cover them until they bloom and soften.

When ready to serve, add the dried fruits and raisins (if using) to the apricot pudding. Divide among small bowls and top with the nuts.

400 g (14 oz) apricot leather

1 litre (4 cups) boiling water

60 g (¼ cup) caster (superfine) sugar

40 g (⅓ cup) cornflour (cornstarch)

1 teaspoon orange blossom water

1 tablespoon rose water

100 g (3½ oz) dried apricots

100 g (3½ oz) dried prunes

100–150 g (3½–5 oz) mix of raisins (optional), pistachios, almonds, cashews and pine nuts

PANCAKES STUFFED WITH ASHTA OR WALNUTS
Atayef Ashta & Atayef Joz

MAKES ABOUT 20

Another scent- and food-related memory dear to my heart is of *atayef* on Saint Barbara's Day on December 3. I'd be coming home from school along the alleyways late after dark, and along the way the smell of these pancakes and the other aromatic desserts flavoured with anise and orange blossom water made on St. Barbara's Day would fill the whole neighbourhood. *Atayef* are typical on this day and usually the *ashta*-filled variety is more common. Like most Lebanese desserts, the sweetness comes from the sugar syrup offered on the side.

Rafiq Al Rachidi is a shop in Beirut that sells this dessert, among other excellent pastries and products, to restaurants. They're also probably the most known and trusted source for *moghrabieh* pearls. During Ramadan, they will have a 30-cm (12-in) *atayef* dough stuffed with walnuts and baked or fried then drizzled with syrup, ready to be served. You can try to make that version using the following recipe, but it's nicer to have small bite-sized portions even if it takes a little more time.

Mix the flour, water, yeast and sugar in a bowl until fully incorporated, then leave to rest for 20 minutes.

When you are ready to cook, mix the baking powder into the batter.

Heat a wide frying pan or a flat skillet over a medium heat and wipe with a little bit of oil. Scoop 2 tablespoons of the batter into the pan and spread in an even layer around 10–12 cm (4–5 in) in diameter and cook on one side only for around 2 minutes until the whole surface is covered in bubbles and the middle has just barely turned from wet to firm. Do not spread the batter further or roll the pan, as that will make the edges thin and crispy and will stop them from adhering at the next stage. Remove and place on a tray and cover with a clean dish towel. Repeat the process with the remaining batter.

Let the pancakes cool for 1–2 hours before filling – this will help them soften and become pliable. Otherwise, cover in clingfilm (plastic wrap) and store for 1 day in the refrigerator.

60 ml (¼ cup) vegetable oil or melted butter, for frying

1 x recipe quantity Syrup (recipe in *Nammoura*, page 162), for brushing

For the pancake batter

200 g (1⅓ cup) plain (all-purpose) flour

400 ml (generous 1½ cups) water

½ teaspoon dried yeast

1 teaspoon caster (superfine) sugar

2 teaspoons baking powder

Fillings
(each recipe makes enough to fill a full batch of pancakes)

For *Atayef Ashta*

½ x recipe quantity *Ashta* (see page 219)

30 g (¼ cup) nibbed pistachios

orange blossom petal jam, to decorate

For *Atayef Joz*

100 g (1 cup) shelled walnuts

3 tablespoons caster (superfine) sugar

2 teaspoons orange blossom water

2 teaspoons rose water

DESSERTS

174

For the *Atayef Ashta:* Prepare the *ashta* for the filling (see page 219). Blitz the pistachios in a food processor until finely ground. Set aside.

Take about 1 teaspoon of the *ashta* and place it onto one quarter of a pancake, seeping a small tail of filling towards the middle. Fold the pancake over and pinch the empty side between the tips of your fingers until you create a cone shape. Dip the exposed filling into the ground pistachios and arrange the *atayef* on a serving a plate in a circular shape. Top with the orange blossom petal jam and serve immediately.

For the *Atayef Joz:* Preheat the oven to 180°C (350°F/gas 4).

Blitz the walnuts in a food processor until finely crushed. Add the sugar and aromatic waters and mix to combine.

Take each pancake and fill with half to a full teaspoon of the walnut filling and fold over and pinch the sides between your fingers. Brush the edges with a little water to help them stick if they have dried out too much.

Arrange the *atayef* on a baking sheet and brush both sides with oil or butter. Bake for 20 minutes, flipping them halfway through.

Remove from the oven and, while they are still hot, brush or drizzle with the syrup. Let cool.

Serve with coffee. Both types of *atayef* should be served with more syrup on the side for those who love their sweets to be a bit EXTRA. Traditionally, *atayef joz* are deep-fried then dropped into the syrup while hot, which you can totally do too – no judgement!

Pictured overleaf.

WALNUT BAKLAVA
Hadef

During the month of Ramadan, Rafiq Al Rachidi stops selling *knefe* and other desserts and the shop is filled instead with *atayef* and this type of *baklava* – *hadef* – which is not found in any other month of the year. While the shape might be common in other countries, the walnut filling is not. Typically, *baklava* made with filo pastry in Lebanon are filled with cashews, and *katayfi baklava* (made with a vermicelli-like dough) are filled with pistachios. Since *hadef* are only available for 28 days of the year, their arrival is hotly anticipated.

Pulse the walnuts in a food processor until finely chopped. Transfer to a bowl, add 1 tablespoon of the sugar and the rose water and knead until the mixture holds together when squeezed. Leave to marinate for 2 hours.

Preheat the oven to 200°C (400°F/gas 6). Brush the bottom and sides of a deep 22 x 30 cm (9 x 12 in) baking pan with the melted butter/ghee.

Divide the pastry sheets into 2 portions. Take a few sheets from the first portion and place them at the bottom of the baking pan and brush them with butter/ghee. Add more sheets and brush until you have used up the first portion. Don't brush the last sheet, but sprinkle ½ tablespoon of sugar over the top instead – this will help the filling adhere to the pastry sheet. Tip in the walnut filling and press with your palm until tightly packed. Sprinkle with the final ½ tablespoon of sugar.

Repeat the pastry-butter layering process again until the second portion of pastry is used up. Don't brush the top sheet with butter. Cover with a piece of clingfilm (plastic wrap) and press firmly with your palms until well compacted. Remove the clingfilm and use a sharp knife to make diagonal cuts to create lozenges of *baklava*. Brush with the remaining butter.

Bake for 10 minutes without opening the oven door, then reduce the heat to 180°C (350°F/gas 4) and bake for a further 25–30 minutes until golden.

Meanwhile, prepare the syrup by mixing the sugar and water in a saucepan and stirring until it has dissolved. Boil for 5 minutes, then remove from the heat and flavour with lemon juice, rose water and orange blossom water.

Once the *baklava* is out of the oven, douse it with all of the syrup. Let cool completely before cutting and serving. Store in an airtight container.

250 g (2½ cups) shelled walnuts

2 tablespoons caster (superfine) sugar

2 tablespoons rose water

100 g (generous ⅓ cup) butter, melted (or substitute half of it with ghee)

250 g (9 oz) filo (phyllo) pastry sheets

For the syrup

350 g (1½ cups) caster (superfine) sugar

120 ml (½ cup) water

1 teaspoon freshly squeezed lemon juice

2 tablespoons orange blossom water

2 tablespoons rose water

ASHTA ICE CREAM
Booza Ashta

You can group all the ice creams, gelatos and frozen desserts of the world into one category and put Lebanese *ashta* ice cream into a category all of its own. It is made with salep powder, a flavouring and starchy thickening agent that gives the ice cream a firm consistency and resistance to melting quickly. Another factor that makes this ice cream special is the technique used to make it. After the ingredients are mixed, it is pounded in a large mortar and pestle over ice. Beating it repeatedly creates the texture and freezes the mixture with the least crystallisation possible. For serving in shops, the ice cream is shaped into an inverted cone and covered generously in ground pistachios, while the take-home version is shaped like a Swiss roll layered with the nuts.

In a pestle and mortar, pound the mastic with the sugar into a fine powder.

In a saucepan off the heat, mix together the milk, salep powder, mastic powder and simple syrup, whisking until combined. Set over a medium heat, bring to the boil and cook until it starts to thicken. Remove from the heat and allow to cool slightly.

When slightly cooled, add the rose water and orange blossom water, then mix in the *ashta* until incorporated. Let cool to room temperature, transfer to a freezer-safe container, cover and freeze for 2 hours. (Alternatively, you can churn it in an ice-cream machine at this point, according to the manufacturer's instructions.)

After 2 hours, remove from the freezer and fork through to break up any ice crystals that are forming. Cover and freeze for 1 hour.

After 1 hour, remove and stir again, then freeze for another 2 hours.

Remove from the freezer, cut into pieces and blend in a blender or food processor. Take care – the mixture will be thick.

Lay a large sheet of clingfilm (plastic wrap) on a work surface and sprinkle over the ground pistachios in an even layer. Scoop the ice cream from the blender (or direct from the ice-cream machine) on top of the pistachios in an even layer. Working quickly, use the clingfilm to roll the ice cream up into a log. Twist the sides like a candy wrapper to tighten and firm it up, then freeze again for at least 2 hours before slicing and serving.

2 g (½ teaspoon) mastic (found in Middle Eastern grocers or online)

1 teaspoon granulated sugar

500 ml (2 cups) milk

2 tablespoons salep/sahlab powder (found in Middle Eastern grocers or online)

175 ml (¾ cup) simple syrup (equal parts sugar and water, heated until dissolved, then cooled)

1 tablespoon rose water

1 tablespoon orange blossom water

250 g (1 cup) *Ashta* (page 219)

100–150 g (1–1½ cups) ground pistachios

LEMON SORBET
Bouza A'ala Hamod

1 litre (4 cups) water

450 g (2 cups) caster (superfine) sugar

2 whole lemons (optional)

500 ml (2 cups) freshly squeezed
    lemon juice (from about 14 lemons
    – why not hollow out a few and use
    them for presentation)

2 tablespoons orange blossom water,
    or to taste

There is one man in Beirut who I believe makes a perfect lemon sorbet. His name is Mitri Moussa, commonly known by the name of his father who opened the shop, Hanna Mitri. Mitri inherited the shop from his father after being his right-hand man for years, even while he maintained an office job. The shop was located in an old building that was under threat of collapse, but that somehow added to the appeal of the shop. Mitri is always in the shop with his mother and they will share the story of how the shop and the building survived bullets and bombs during the civil war, with scars on the walls and the oven they use to bake *ma'amoul*. It was only on August 4 2020, with the explosions at the port, that the building finally started to collapse, forcing Mitri to move out of the shop his family have owned since 1946. Mitri moved his shop into a more stable building a few minutes away and is still making the most delicious ice creams and sorbets in town. His lemon sorbet has the right balance of sweetness and tartness and is so light and refreshing. I've tried to replicate the recipe here, but you really have to visit Mitri to try his other incredibly fresh flavours.

Start by mixing the water and sugar in a saucepan and bring to a simmer until the sugar is dissolved. Set aside to cool.

If adding whole lemons, zest them (reserving the zest in an airtight container) and cut them into slices to remove the seeds, then place in a food processor. Pulse the lemons along with the lemon juice until well blended. Add the cooled sugar syrup and orange blossom water and pulse again to combine.

Pour the mixture into a freezer-safe container and freeze for at least 4 hours or overnight.

Once frozen, remove from the container and cut into pieces that will fit in the food processor. Blend until smooth and super creamy. Add more orange blossom water, to taste, and the reserved lemon zest and mix again.

Return the mixture to the freezer container and freeze for 1–2 hours until set, then serve. If you like, for a fun presentation, pour the mixture into the hollowed-out skins of the lemons and freeze before serving.

DRINKS

You can always count on a dark cup of coffee or a sweet cup of tea, but there's more to Lebanese beverages. A visit to a *Mouneh* shop will amaze you with all the types of sweet syrups, made from fruits or herbs, and distilled waters, beyond rose and orange blossom. There are also all the wild herbs and plants that people have long used for medicinal purposes, and still do. Most people, for example, still associate sage with old grandmothers and tummy aches. But have you had it in an alcoholic cocktail? I love a wild gimlet with gin and sage.

In this chapter, I've collected a selection of rather easy drinks to make at home. They can be enjoyed as drinks on their own, or form part of a cocktail, if you're feeling adventurous. Try the syrups diluted with sparkling water with ice or pair them with a spirit that complements the flavours. Mulberry syrup (page 202), as well as rose syrup, works well with *arak*, and is very popular in bars and restaurants in Beirut. *Einer* (page 198) is great over ice as well as warm in a mug, maybe with a splash of bourbon to complement the sweet cinnamon flavour.

Jallab (page 194) is a great drink for breaking fast, and is typically consumed during Ramadan. It can also work well over crushed or shaved ice like a snow cone. I've also tried mixing it with spirits – be adventurous and don't limit yourself.

There are two bars in Beirut that I really love for their sense of adventure in cocktails. Anise in Mar Mikhayel, a young and hip street with restaurants, bars and art shops in every nook and cranny, and Ferdinand in Hamra, an area that used to hold the crown that Mar Mikhayel now holds. Their use of local ingredients in drinks is always fascinating, and everything from za'atar and sage to dried fruits and locally made spirits features on their menus.

SALEP MILK DRINK
Sahlab

Sahlab was originally made using salep powder, which is ground *orchis* tuber, from the orchid family. It is mixed with milk and sugar and heated until thickened into a delicious drink or pudding, which is often served for winter breakfasts or as an evening snack. *Sahlab* drink was popular in England around the beginning of the nineteenth century. Known as 'saloop', it lost popularity when tax reductions made tea more affordable. The extract is also the main ingredient in *ashta* ice cream, or *booza*, as it gives a unique flavour and strength to the dessert.

Nowadays, most of the pure salep powder comes from one area in Turkey, but there's such high demand for it that the orchid could become extinct. For this reason, pure salep powder might be hard to find. If unavailable, I have given you a version of the recipe with cornflour (cornstarch), which closely replicates the drink.

Pound the mastic and 1 tablespoon of the sugar in a mortar and pestle to a fine powder. Adding sugar will help grind the mastic more easily.

If you are using pure salep powder: Pour all the milk into a saucepan. Add the salep and ground mastic along with the rest of the sugar and whisk until dissolved. Place over a medium–high heat and whisk or stir constantly until thickened.

If you are using cornflour: Pour 750 ml (3 cups) of the milk into a saucepan and add the ground mastic along with the rest of the sugar. Place over a medium–high heat, bring to the boil, then reduce the heat to low.

Dissolve the cornflour in the remaining 250 ml (1 cup) cold milk and add it to the saucepan. Stir constantly until the mixture thickens.

To finish: Divide among 4 mugs or glasses, sprinkle with cinnamon and garnish with a cinnamon stick. Serve with sweet Lebanese sesame breadsticks on the side.

1 g (¼ teaspoon) mastic (found in Middle Eastern grocers or online)

4 tablespoons sugar

1 litre (4 cups) cold milk

1 tablespoon salep/sahlab powder (found in Middle Eastern grocers or online), or to taste, OR 4 tablespoons cornflour (cornstarch)

pinch of ground cinnamon

4 cinnamon sticks, to garnish

To serve

sweet Lebanese sesame breadsticks or cookies (*kaak*)

ROSE-SCENTED GRAPE SYRUP WITH NUTS
Jallab

Jallab is a unique product. During Ramadan, there's a particular ad jingle for it that starts playing all month long on TV, that most Lebanese, if not all, know by heart. Carts with glass dispensers filled to the top with *jallab* and tamarind drinks and pure liquorice extract start roaming the streets around *Iftar* time, and people from the neighbourhood gather around to grab their drinks before the *Adhan*, the sunset call for prayer announcing the end of the day's fasting.

Commercial *jallab* syrups are filled with sugar and artificial colourings and flavourings and much less of the good stuff that brings nutrition to the body after a long day of fasting. This recipe is made with no added sugar or added colouring. You may, if you prefer, use a few drops of red food colouring mixed with a drop of black food colouring to achieve the classic rosewood colour of *jallab*. You may also use date syrup or molasses if you can't find grape molasses.

Smoking the liquid is essential as it infuses the rose flavour into it. It's okay if you can't find rose frankincense – try using other natural incense resins, but not the compressed incense sticks or cones.

250 g (2 cups) sultanas (golden raisins)

1 litre (4 cups) boiling water

300 g (scant 1 cup) grape molasses

1 small piece of charcoal

3 tiny (lentil-sized) pieces of rose frankincense resin (found in Middle Eastern grocers or online)

4 tablespoons rose water

To serve (per glass)

1 teaspoon pine nuts

1 tablespoon blanched almonds

1 tablespoon cashews

cold water, to top up

crushed ice

Put the sultanas in a bowl, pour over the boiling water and leave to soak overnight until they rehydrate and puff up.

Pour the sultanas along with their soaking liquid into a blender or food processor and blitz well, then strain them through a cheesecloth (muslin) or a lined strainer set over a bowl and squeeze out as as much liquid as possible (discard the pulp, but reserve the collected juice).

In a saucepan with a lid, mix the collected juices with the grape molasses. Bring to a simmer and cook for 15 minutes, then turn off the heat.

Meanwhile, light the charcoal and let it come to red hot.

Carefully place a heatproof bowl in the middle of the syrup in the pan. If necessary, place a shot glass underneath to support the bowl to avoid it touching the syrup or risk it being submerged. Carefully place the hot coal in the bowl and sprinkle the tiny pieces of frankincense on the coal. Immediately cover the pot with a lid and allow the syrup to infuse with the rose scent for 5–7 minutes, or until the smoke subsides. Carefully remove the coal and bowl from the pan.

Finally, stir the rose water into the infused syrup.

Store in a bottle in the refrigerator for up to 2 weeks.

Ahead of serving, soak the nuts for garnishing in a little water for 1–2 hours until softened.

To serve, pour 4 tablespoons of the syrup into each glass. Top up with 4 tablespoons of cold water and stir until mixed. Fill each glass with crushed ice, then top up with more cold water. Garnish with the soaked nuts and serve immediately.

Pictured overleaf.

CARAWAY-&-CINNAMON-SPICED DRINK
Einer

Traditionally, *einer* is a perfect winter drink. It's infused with warming spices and is enough to keep you warm and toasty for the night. The flavours are similar to those of *Meghli* (page 168) since both rely heavily on cinnamon and caraway. For my version of the drink, I add cornflour (cornstarch) to thicken the mix since I want to have a slightly thick drink, similar to the texture of hot chocolate. But feel free to skip it. It's also great served chilled over ice. I could imagine it with bourbon or whisky or rum in a sweet and warm cocktail, or a spiced version of a Hot Toddy.

Mix the water, sugar and the spices in a saucepan. Bring to the boil, then reduce the heat and simmer for 15 minutes.

Mix the cornflour with a little cold water, then stir into the spice infusion. Stir constantly until the mixture thickens slightly.

Strain and serve in glasses, topped with chopped walnuts.

Alternatively, you can chill it in the refrigerator after straining and serve over ice as a refreshing drink with warm flavours.

1 litre (4 cups) water

4 tablespoons sugar

2 tablespoons ground cinnamon

1 tablespoon ground caraway

2 cinnamon sticks

3 tablespoons cornflour (cornstarch)

100 g (generous ¾ cup) shelled walnuts, chopped, to serve

YOGHURT DRINK
Ayran

400 g (generous 1½ cups) plain yoghurt
500 ml (2 cups) chilled water
a pinch of sea salt

Fresh *ayran* relies on good yoghurt. We use the slightly sour kind, since it adds a nice kick to this drink. *Ayran* is popular in many Middle Eastern countries and it goes by different names, but it is virtually the same product: yoghurt, water and salt. We love it with *Lahm Baajine* (page 51) and other meat pastries, or on its own as a refreshing and nutritious drink.

Place everything in a blender and blitz until frothy. Serve chilled.

Pictured on page 55.

SYRUPS

A great rule of thumb: whatever is produced seasonally in this land has a way to be preserved, whether it's pickled in brine, sun-dried or fermented. Syrups are basically fruit juices preserved or infused in simple sugar syrup to increase the longevity and taste of fruits and aromatics for seasons to come. Basically, anything can be made into a syrup. Think mulberries, cherries, rose, mint, etc. I have even made apple syrup from peels that were to be discarded. Let your creativity run wild.

Traditionally, these are served as *dyafé*, the offering made to visiting guests, diluted with water to the desired consistency and flavour and topped with ice for a refreshing drink on hot days. Forget the instant powder drink or fizzy drinks with artificial ingredients and colours — let's go back to traditional methods. Don't limit yourself to traditional serving suggestions though. These can be an excellent base for alcoholic cocktails. *Arak* with mulberry or rose syrup is a great example. Gin and vodka work just as well with syrups. Try the Bitter Orange Syrup opposite to make an Old Fashioned, a Manhattan, or a Martini!

BITTER ORANGE SYRUP
Sharab El Bou Sfeir

1.5 kg (3 lb 5 oz) bitter oranges, washed, zested and peeled

about 1.3 kg (6 cups) granulated sugar (see method)

To serve (per glass)
crushed ice

cold water, to top up

This syrup is a by-product of the bitter oranges that come into season in the middle of winter here in Lebanon. As they are being harvested, new blossoms start opening waiting to be pollinated and their scent fills the surroundings. There are a couple of streets in Beirut that are particularly lined with these trees, in Monot and Achrafieh. The white petals and the fresh citrussy smell announce the change of season to a warmer one.

The bitter orange rinds are used to make a classic preserve, while the juice is boiled with sugar and preserved in bottles for a refreshing drink in warmer weather. Before you squeeeze the oranges, make sure to wash, zest and then peel them. I infuse the zest in olive oil over a very low heat, strain it and store it in bottles to use as body oil. The zest can also be mixed with salt to make a citrusy salt seasoning or home-made body or lip scrubs. The rinds can then be used to make the delicious preserve (see page 214).

First, juice the oranges and measure the amount of juice they produce. Double that figure to calculate the amount of sugar you need. I got about 750 ml (3 cups) juice from 1.5 kg of fruit, so I needed 6 cups of sugar.

Combine the juice and sugar in a heavy-based saucepan and boil, stirring occasionally, until the sugar is dissolved and the syrup has thickened.

Let it cool slightly, then very carefully pour into sterilised bottles (see page 224) and seal. They will keep in a dry place for up to a year.

To serve, pour around 2 tablespoons of syrup into a glass, top with cold water and stir. Adjust for taste and sweetness. Fill with ice and serve.

MULBERRY SYRUP
Sharab El Tout

MAKES ABOUT 1.2 LITRES
(4¾ CUPS)

Black mulberries grow widely in Lebanon, especially at higher altitudes. We call them *Toot Shami*, or Levantine berries. These purple, almost black, berries are tart with a fruity punch and are the best type for syrup making.

I have a particular childhood memory of making mulberry syrup. Mom had bought a large amount of mulberries and I volunteered to help press them for syrup. She gave me a fine mesh bag and started filling it with batches of mulberries that I would squeeze until no juice would come out. My hands were all red and purple from the sweet and sticky juice and I loved every minute of it. It was a moment I was dying to repeat and it was only because of writing this book that I decided to buy mulberries again to make my own syrup instead of buying the syrup from a friend. It's a visually gruesome scene, but for me an intense food moment that I enjoy and look forward to repeating. I don't mind having red-stained hands for a couple of hours.

We love to serve this prepared drink over ice, or to freeze it in cups and shave with a metal spoon like a granita. It was our version of home-made fruit popsicles.

Blitz the mulberries in a blender or food processor, then strain through a cheesecloth (muslin) or lined strainer set over a bowl and squeeze out as much liquid as you can (if not too gritty, the pulp can be reserved and used in a smoothie, or folded into ice cream or a sweet dough).

Weigh or measure the collected juice and weigh out the equivalent amount of sugar.

Place the juice and sugar in a large saucepan, stir well and bring to the boil. Remove and discard the froth that forms on the top with a slotted spoon or a small strainer. Reduce the heat and simmer, stirring occasionally, for 40–50 minutes until the mixture thickens slightly into a syrup.

Let it cool slightly, then pour into sterilised bottles and seal. Properly sealed, the syrup will keep for up to a year.

To serve, fill a glass with 3 tablespoons of the syrup and top with cold water and ice. Taste – if it tastes weak, add more syrup, stir and serve.

1 kg (7 cups) mulberries

about 800 g (3½ cups) caster (superfine) sugar (see method)

To serve (per glass)

crushed ice

cold water, to top up

BASICS

ZA'ATAR SPICE MIX
Za'atar Makhlout

EACH RECIPE MAKES 1 X
700-ML (24-FL OZ) JAR

I love to use this spice mix in a large wrap, brushed with olive oil to make the za'atar stick, filled with cucumber, mint, olives, tomato and lettuce. You can also sprinkle it on Labneh (page 216), over salads, inside a *Ka'ak* (page 56), or mix it with olive oil for delicious *Manouche* (page 46).

In a dry pan, briefly toast the sesame seeds until golden and fragrant. Leave to cool, then mix the sesame seeds with the sumac, oregano/za'atar and salt. Store in an airtight jar.

- 100 g (¾ cup) sesame seeds
- 80 g (¾ cup) sumac
- 50 g (1½ cups) dried ground oregano or Lebanese wild thyme (what we know as za'atar – if you can find some)
- ½ teaspoon salt

SYRIAN-STYLE ZA'ATAR
Za'atar Halabi

This nutty variation hails from Aleppo. Use on top of Labneh (page 216) or salads, or mix with some olive oil as a flavourful dip for bread.

In a dry pan, lightly toast the pistachios and walnuts to bring out their flavour, then allow to cool. Grind in a food processor until fine but not completely powdery.

In the same pan, briefly toast the sesame seeds until golden and fragrant. Leave to cool, then mix everything together. Store in an airtight jar.

- 25 g (3 tablespoons) shelled pistachios
- 25 g (¼ cup) walnut halves
- 50 g (scant ½ cup) sesame seeds
- 50 g (1½ cups) dried ground oregano or Lebanese wild thyme
- 50 g (scant ½ cup) sumac
- 15 g (2½ tablespoons) ground cumin
- ½ teaspoon salt

SWEET & SPICY ZA'ATAR
Za'atar Helou w Harr

Perfect for topping dips, salads, or for sprinkling on buttered toast.

In a dry pan, briefly toast the sesame seeds until golden and fragrant. Leave to cool, then mix with the rest of the ingredients. Store in an airtight jar.

- 3½ tablespoons sesame seeds
- 50 g (1½ cups) dried ground oregano or Lebanese wild thyme
- 2 tablespoons each of dried barberries and dried cranberries, chopped
- 3½ tablespoons sumac
- 2 tablespoons dried chilli (red pepper) flakes

BASIC PILAF
Riz Mfalfal

The base for any Beiruti pilaf recipe is this simple, but perfectly cooked, combination of rice and vermicelli noodles. Toasting the vermicelli until golden adds a nutty flavour and I like to toast the rice in the oil and butter for the same reason.

Back in the old days, long before rice was introduced to the Levantine diet, this pilaf was made with burghul, since it was the local crop and it had more nutritional benefits. Some people still prefer a burghul pilaf instead of rice alongside traditional stews. My grandma told me that, before vermicelli was commercially available, to pass the time on long nights, the family would gather and roll pieces of unleavened dough into long, thin strands and toss them in a basket to be dried later to make vermicelli. If a man wanted to get to know a girl from a certain family, he'd ask to join one of those nights of vermicelli-making as a way to see her and maybe talk to her in a family-approved setting.

Heat the oil and butter in a saucepan over a medium heat, add the vermicelli and cook, stirring, until golden. Stir in the rice, then pour in the water or stock. Season with salt and bring to the boil, then reduce the heat, cover with a lid, and simmer for 15–20 minutes until the water is completely absorbed.

Turn off the heat and fluff the rice with a fork or stir with a wooden spoon, then put the lid back on the pan and let rest for 5 minutes before serving.

Note: Some people prefer the pilaf with short-grain rice, although it is a little clumpy compared to long-grain. Wash the rice well until the water runs clear and slightly reduce the quantity of cooking water. The pilaf can also be made without vermicelli, using the same proportions.

1 tablespoon vegetable oil

1 tablespoon butter

60 g (⅔ cup) crumbled vermicelli noodles (alternatively, you can use no.1 spaghetti)

280 g (1½ cups) long-grain rice, rinsed

500 ml (2 cups) water or stock

1 teaspoon fine salt

TAHINI SAUCE
Tarator

135 g (½ cup) tahini

60 ml (¼ cup) water

60 ml (¼ cup) freshly squeezed
lemon juice

½ teaspoon fine salt

Now a trendy ingredient in the Western pantry, tahini has existed for centuries in this part of the world. There are mentions of the cultivation of sesame in ancient Mesopotamia 3,500 years ago. Tahini is made from crushing or grinding sesame seeds. *Tarator* is a sauce made by adding water, lemon juice and salt to tahini. Serve with grilled or fried fish, falafel, or roasted or fried cauliflower, or just dip bread into it, as I do!

Pour the tahini and water into a bowl and whisk together until incorporated. Don't worry if the tahini splits – keep whisking and it will come together again. Add the lemon juice and salt and whisk until combined, then taste and adjust – add more lemon juice if you like it more lemony; more water if you want a runnier texture.

CORIANDER & GARLIC PESTO
Salset Kezbra w Toom

200 g (7 oz) garlic

300 g (10½ oz) fresh coriander (cilantro),
both leaves and stems

1 tablespoon sea salt

3 tablespoons freshly squeezed
lemon juice

250 ml (1 cup) olive oil

Beirutis love this. It is used in so many recipes and is perfect with roasted veggies, slathered on bread, in stir-fries, with chicken or with fish and in marinades. It is often stir-fried in olive oil to release its flavours before mixing into stews. Having a jar in the fridge always comes in handy.

Place the garlic, coriander, salt and lemon juice in a food processor and blitz until very finely chopped. With the motor still running, drizzle in the olive oil through the feed tube until the sauce emulsifies.

Store in small jars in the refrigerator, covered in a thin layer of olive oil, for up to 2 weeks or freeze in tubs or an ice-cube tray until needed.

PRESERVES

With a generally moderate climate, Lebanon enjoys four fantastic seasons. And with those seasons, nature blessed us with an abundance of produce to savour. To make everything last the longest time possible, people cook many items in sugar and preserve them in jars. You've probably never heard of sweet eggplant preserve, but it exists. Similarly, preserved pumpkin chunks, or even preserved unripe walnuts, prepared when their shells are still soft and edible. Villagers process whatever comes out of their land so that nothing is wasted. All the produce that is blemished, or otherwise ugly, is chopped and made into a jam.

Beirutis and city residents rely on relatives in villages to share any extra produce they can give away. Otherwise, they go to markets, typically towards the end of the day, to bargain over whatever produce is left and get a large amount at a reasonable price for making jam.

One vivid memory that I still carry with me is of a midsummer's eve when we were visiting my aunt at dusk. The scene was bluish and the faint light that could still penetrate the house shone on trays of apricot jam that were spread out to dry in the hot day's sun to evaporate any leftover moisture before storing in jars. This method is used when less sugar and a shorter cooking time are used to preserve the colour and fresh taste of the fruits. The scents and sights of that day are ones I can remember to this day. Making jams at home always brings that memory back. My mom and I still try to keep this tradition alive and enjoy the blessings of this home-made product.

Jams and preserves are served either as dessert, with coffee for the afternoon *asrouniyeh* (see feature on page 166), or in a wrap, with butter, white cheese, or a banana.

PLUM JAM
Mrabba el Khoukh

1 kg (2 lb 4 oz) plums, washed and dried

about 800 g (3⅔ cups) granulated white sugar (see method)

1 tablespoon lemon juice

One of my relatives grows plum trees on their land. I raid them from time to time to make jam, as the fruits are often left to get really ripe and almost ruined by the birds. Jam making is not hard. All you have to do is cook the fruits with sugar until the mix thickens. The proportion of sugar to fruit depends on the type of fruit and its sweetness/tartness level. The sweeter the fruit, the less sugar it needs. Some producers in Beirut make jam simply by cooking down the fruits using their natural sugars, but I feel it doesn't produce the same quality of jam.

Before you start, have some sterilised jars (see page 224) ready for filling and place a saucer or metal spoon in the freezer.

Cut the plums in half, twisting them to separate and remove the stones, then cut into quarters and place in a bowl. If the plums are very ripe, this will be messy and they may squash, but it doesn't matter. Once you're done, weigh the plums. You need to add 80 per cent of that weight in sugar.

Weigh out the correct proportion of sugar and add it to the plums, giving them a stir. Cover with a cloth and place in the refrigerator for at least 1 hour, or ideally overnight.

The next day, spoon the contents of the bowl into a large non-reactive (stainless-steel) saucepan and bring to the boil. The mixture will bubble and foam. Use a slotted spoon to skim off and discard the foam. Keep stirring occasionally until the fruits have melted into the juice, the sugar has completely dissolved and the mixture has thickened slightly.

To test whether the jam is ready, take a cold saucer or spoon out of the freezer and drop a small amount of the jam onto them. If the jam doesn't slide off the spoon or plate, and the surface of it wrinkles when pushed gently with a fingertip, then the jam is ready. If the jam is still runny, then it needs more cooking time. Stir in the lemon juice and remove from the heat.

To get a smooth jam, use a hand-held stick blender to very carefully blend the jam until smooth (it will be very hot – take care!). This step is optional.

Spoon the hot jam into the jars, seal, and leave to cool. Store in a cool, dark place. Unopened, it will keep for up to 1 year, but may discolour a little. Once opened, store in the refrigerator.

BITTER ORANGE PRESERVE
Mrabba El Bou Sfeir

In this book, I've tried to document traditional recipes that are fading in popularity and from the public eye. Home-made jams are still trendy products in farmers' markets and fairs, but are less seen in general consumption. This delicious recipe can sub for candy. It's a perfect accompaniment for afternoon coffee (*asrouniyeh*) or served as a post-meal sweet bite, or a nightly nibble. It is made from the rinds of bitter oranges, the juice of which can either made into a syrup (page 201) or used in *Ful* (page 21) or *Kibbeh Arnabiyeh* (page 110).

Zest the bitter oranges to smooth the surface of the rind and remove the essential oils that are found in the zest, then score the rind into segments and carefully peel it away from the fruit. Weigh the rinds and take note of the weight, then measure out the same weight in sugar as the weight of the rinds and set aside.

Roll each piece of rind into a coil, and use a needle and thread to thread the coils together so that they hold their shape. Make 3–4 necklaces of coiled rinds.

Place the rinds in a large saucepan and add enough water to cover. Bring to the boil, then reduce the heat and simmer for 5 minutes, then drain. Place the rinds back in the same pan, add the cloves and cover with the sugar. Leave overnight to infuse.

The next day, add around 250 ml (1 cup) of water to the pan, if needed, so that the rinds are barely covered with liquid and bring to the boil. Reduce the heat and simmer for about 30 minutes until all the sugar is dissolved. Remove from the heat and let cool.

Remove the rinds from the threads and carefully arrange them in sterilised jars (see page 224). Top up each jar with the liquid from the pan. The rinds must be covered in liquid, so if more liquid is needed, add some simple syrup. Close the lids and store until your sweet tooth wants a feeding.

1.5 kg (3 lb 5 oz) bitter oranges

granulated or caster (superfine) sugar (see method for weight)

5 cloves

STRAINED YOGHURT
Labneh

2 kg (8 cups) plain yoghurt
(preferably a little tangy)

1 teaspoon fine salt, or to taste

This tastes amazing in a wrap with vegetables and olive oil, or spread over toasted bread, or as a delicious dip drizzled with plenty of olive oil. It is probably the reason I can't go vegan. There is always a tub of labneh in the refrigerator. We make our labneh at home, and you should, too.

Sometimes, we also make our own yoghurt. We'd get a 5-litre fresh milk container from a farm or nearby vendor and heat it through while watching it closely. They say a watched pot never boils, and that's why you should never leave its side. It should not boil over. Once the milk starts to rise, turn off the heat immediately, otherwise it will burn, and let it cool to lukewarm.

Stir in 4 tablespoons of yoghurt to bring in a good culture of bacteria to start off the new yoghurt. The type of yoghurt you use for the culture determines the quality of yoghurt you're making. Find a Middle Eastern strain of yoghurt, if possible, or borrow a small coffee cup of yoghurt from someone else who makes it, as my mom would do whenever she had run out of it. Put the lid on, cover with a blanket to maintain a stable warm temperature and place in a draught-free location for 8–10 hours, undisrupted. Uncover and refrigerate before using.

Ideally, a clay pot is perfect for making yoghurt as it keeps a stable temperature and the porous clay absorbs the extra moisture, producing a naturally thick and creamy yoghurt.

I vividly remember when, as an 11-year-old boy, Mom used to send me to the end of the street to grab a gallon of fresh milk from Abou Assaad, our neighbour who kept cows and goats. If I ever had to leave the Lebanon, I'd have to find a way to smuggle some dried sheets of yoghurt out, so that I could rehydrate them wherever I go and make the good Lebanese yoghurt that I love. Mom and I always loved the fatty creamy top that forms on top of fresh home-made yoghurt. And, from that same yoghurt, you'll get the best creamy labneh, with its iconic sourness.

Place the yoghurt in a cheesecloth (muslin) or – as we always did – in a clean cotton pillowcase dedicated to labneh-making. Tie the top of the cloth or bag and hang it up (the kitchen tap/faucet is usually ideal for this) or place it in a strainer set over a bowl to catch all the whey. Leave to strain for at least 6 hours or overnight – the longer you leave it, the thicker it gets.

In warm weather you will need to keep it in the refrigerator overnight, but in cold weather, you can safely keep it out for the specified time.

When the strained yoghurt has reached your desired consistency, scoop it into a bowl. Add salt, to taste, and store in the refrigerator.

Note: If you leave it to drain for longer, you should be able to roll it into balls with your hands. Coat the balls in chilli powder, sumac or za'atar and store in a jar covered with olive oil. It's perfect to spread on bread or to crumble over as a salad topper.

WHITE BALADI GOAT'S CHEESE
Jebne Bayda Baladiye

It is one thing to taste new foods, but it's quite different to make them from scratch. During the 2020 Covid-19 quarantine, many people tried to make things at home, especially here in Beirut with constant risks of food shortages. Baladi cheese is a local plain cheese or curdled yoghurt that's strained and seasoned then pressed to shape. Use goat's milk and yoghurt if available, but feel free to use sheep's or cow's milk and yoghurt if that's what you can get. If you'd like to flavour the cheese, add the extra ingredients before pressing the cheese: try paprika, chilli (red pepper) flakes, thyme, rosemary, citrus zest, or whatever you feel like.

Prepare a cheesecloth (muslin) by laying it over a strainer set over a large bowl (or – as we typically do in the Levant – just use a clean pillowcase).

Fill a saucepan with 2 litres (8 cups) of water, add the salt, then bring to the boil to make a salty brine. Set aside to cool.

In a separate large pan, bring the milk to the boil over a medium heat. Keep a close eye on it, so as not to scorch the milk. Gently tip the yoghurt into the hot milk and stir 3–5 times. Reduce the heat and slowly bring to the boil without stirring. As soon as it comes to the boil, remove from the heat and pour the mixture into the cloth-lined strainer.

Squeeze the curds in the cloth and weigh it down with something very heavy (3 kg/6 lb or more). Be creative! Leave the cheese to strain for 15–20 minutes until it reaches your preferred texture.

Remove the cheese from the cloth and cut it into smaller pieces. (You can keep the strained whey and use it in pancakes.) Place the cheese pieces into an airtight container and cover with the brine. Let it stand for 3 hours or overnight in the refrigerator before eating.

The cheese will keep well in the refrigerator, covered in its brine, for 2–3 weeks.

4–5 tablespoons salt
2 kg (10 cups) goat's milk
2 kg (8 cups) goat's yoghurt

ASHTA CLOTTED CREAM
Ashta

1 litre (4 cups) full-fat (whole) milk

70 g (generous ½ cup) cornflour
(cornstarch)

35 g (3 tablespoons) semolina

250 g (generous 1 cup) cottage cheese
or ricotta

1 teaspoon rose water

1 teaspoon orange blossom water

Ashta is the Lebanese version of clotted cream – perfect for stuffing
Atayef (page 174) or for making a tray of *Ma'amoul Ashta* (page 165).
It is also delicious simply topped with honey or fruits. This recipe is one
of my shortcut versions, as the real thing is too much effort – it works just
as well.

Mix the milk, cornflour (cornstarch) and semolina in a saucepan until
incorporated. Place the pan over a medium heat and stir the mixture until it
comes to the boil and starts to thicken. Remove from the heat and stir in the
cheese, rose water and orange blossom water.

Pour the mixture into a container and cover the surface with clingfilm
(plastic wrap) to prevent a skin forming. Allow it to cool to room
temperature before refrigerating for up to a week.

INDEX

Published in 2021 by Smith Street Books
Naarm | Melbourne | Australia
smithstreetbooks.com

ISBN: 978-1-925811-69-8

Publisher: Emily Preece-Morrison
Internal designer: Georgie Hewitt
Cover designer: George Saad
Food photographers: Liz and Max Haarala Hamilton
Food stylist: Valerie Berry
Prop stylist: Aya Nishimura
Location Photographer: Hisham Assaad
Proofreader: Vicky Orchard
Indexer: Vanessa Bird

Printed & bound in China by C&C Offset Printing Co., Ltd.

Book 184
10 9 8 7 6 5 4 3 2 1

To sterilise glass jars: Wash jars and lids in a dishwasher or plenty of hot, soapy water. Rinse thoroughly, then place upside-down on a baking sheet lined with baking paper and dry for 10 minutes in an oven preheated to 180°C (350°F/ gas 4). Handle with care.

Acknowledgements

To Beirut, the city that has given me incredible memories and experiences, and enough heartaches and traumas to last a lifetime. Writing a cookbook in the middle of both global and local storms was tiring. Despite it all, I am proud to have finally produced this book so we can celebrate the city through food.

I am a food lover, not a culinary school graduate (nor dropout!). I love food, not just making or eating it, but all the culture, stories and history behind it. I fell in love with food just from growing up surrounded by good food. Sharing food and stories is one of my favourite activities.

This book is a celebration of Beiruti food and culture. The future is not something we can be sure about: lots of restaurants are closing, access to ingredients is challenging, and home cooking is based on availability and purchase power. But what we are sure of is that these recipes will live on, in the same way that they have lived for ages and have been passed on and developed. Documenting these recipes is what I intended to do, in case we forgot that we used to put pine nuts in our *kibbeh* stuffing.

Developing this book wouldn't have been possible without the support and advice of my family. My mom's patience and generosity in sharing and cooking the recipes are incomparable. My dad and sisters had to go through a military schedule of recipes and repeated recipes throughout the developing and testing phase, and hours of waiting for me to take photos of the food before digging in. Iffat, a Beiriti friend and tour-guide colleague, and my friend Hanine helped with curating recipes and shared their own dishes, stories and food memories that shaped the early drafts of the book. Bethany Kehdy has been a great support since the conception of this book. Karl, George and Sara were there when I needed to discuss, fact-check or proofread.

To my support system: the members of my clown family at Clown Me In. If it weren't for the time we shared together, be it meeting online or in person, when possible, taking to the streets to protest as clowns, rehearsing, and performing after the Beirut port explosion, I wouldn't have stayed sane.

I'm also grateful for the team who worked behind the scenes to get this book out and were patient with me during the toughest time Lebanon has been through. I am thankful to Paul McNally, the publisher at Smith Street Books in Australia, Emily Preece-Morrison, my publisher and commissioning editor in the UK, and all the wonderful people who made the book look amazing and recreated the recipes as faithfully as possible.